KU-268-736

Praise for *Leading on Empty:*

"Having experienced burnout personally earlier in my career I can attest to all Wayne has written, and especially to the fact that out of such a fire can come spiritual growth and maturity. I particularly want to encourage young pastors and Christian leaders who are just starting out in their ministries to devour this book and follow its wise counsel."

—Archibald D. Hart, Ph.D., FPPR.
Senior Professor of Psychology and Dean Emeritus, Graduate School of Psychology, Fuller Theological Seminary

———

"Sooner or later, we all find ourselves trying to lead on empty. It's a tough place to be. But the wisdom, transparency, and godly advice Wayne offers in these pages can spare us the grief. He shows how to keep the tank from running dry—or how to refill it if it's gone empty. If you're in ministry, you need to read this book."

—Larry Osborne
Senior Pastor, North Coast Church, Vista, CA

Books by Wayne Cordeiro
From Bethany House Publishers

The Divine Mentor

Leading on Empty

WAYNE CORDEIRO

LEADING ON EMPTY

REFILLING YOUR TANK
AND RENEWING YOUR PASSION

BETHANYHOUSE
Minneapolis, Minnesota

Leading on Empty
Copyright © 2009
Wayne Cordeiro

Cover design by R-29

Unless otherwise identified, Scripture quotations are taken from the NEW AMERI-CAN STANDARD BIBLE,® Copyright © The Lockman Foundation 1960, 1962, 1963, 1968, 1971, 1972, 1973, 1975, 1977, 1995 by International Bible Society. Used by permission. (www.Lockman.org)
Scripture quotations identified ESV are from The Holy Bible, English Standard Version, copyright © 2001 by Crossway Bibles, a division of Good News Publishers. Used by permission. All rights reserved.
Scripture quotations identified GNT are from the Good News Translation—Second Edition. Copyright © 1992 by American Bible Society. Used by permission.
Scripture quotations identified NIV are from the HOLY BIBLE, NEW INTERNA-TIONAL VERSION.® Copyright © 1973, 1978, 1984 by International Bible Society. Used by permission of Zondervan Publishing House. All rights reserved.
Scripture quotations indentified NKJV are from the New King James Version of the Bible. Copyright © 1979, 1980, 1982 by Thomas Nelson, Inc. Used by permission. All rights reserved.
Scripture quotations identified NLT are from the Holy Bible, New Living Translation, copyright © 1996, 2004. Used by permission of Tyndale House Publishers, Inc., Wheaton, Illinois 60189. All rights reserved.
Scripture quotations identified TEV are from the Bible in Today's English Version (Good News Bible). Copyright © American Bible Society 1966, 1971, 1976, 1992.
Scripture quotations identified TLB are from the The Living Bible © 1971 owned by assignment by Illinois Regional Bank N.A. (trustee). Used by permission of Tyndale House Publishers, Inc., Wheaton, IL 60189. All rights reserved.

All rights reserved. No part of this publication may be reproduced, stored in a retrieval system, or transmitted in any form or by any means—electronic, mechanical, photocopying, recording, or otherwise—without the prior written permission of the publisher. The only exception is brief quotations in printed reviews.

Published by Bethany House Publishers
11400 Hampshire Avenue South
Bloomington, Minnesota 55438

Bethany House Publishers is a division of
Baker Publishing Group, Grand Rapids, Michigan.

Printed in the United States of America

ISBN 978-0-7642-0646-7 (International Trade Paper)

In keeping with biblical principles of creation stewardship, Baker Publishing Group advocates the responsible use of our natural resources. As a member of the Green Press Initiative, our company uses recycled paper when possible. The text paper of this book is comprised of 30% post-consumer waste.

green press
INITIATIVE

The Library of Congress has cataloged the hardcover edition as follows:

Cordeiro, Wayne.
    Leading on empty : refilling your tank and renewing your passion / Wayne Cordeiro.
        p. cm.
    Includes bibliographical references.
    Summary: "Practical help and encouragement for pastors experiencing burnout and depression"—Provided by publisher.
    ISBN 978-0-7642-0350-3 (hardcover : alk. paper)   1. Clergy—Job Stress.   2. Burn out (Psychology)—Religious aspects—Christianity.   3. Clergy—Mental health.   4. Depression, Mental—Religious aspects—Christianity.   5. Cordeiro, Wayne.   I. Title.
    BV 4398.C67   2009
    253'.2—dc22

                                                                          2008051061

Contents

Foreword

by Bob Buford

Ambition is a good thing. Hard work is a good thing. Leisure, rest, and play are good things. But there are limits to each. Let me tell you what has drawn me up short, got me thinking a lot about boundaries and limits. This is a story of two good men, men whose work I know and respect—virtuous men whose lives have been spent serving God's purposes and serving others. We have a ceaseless barrage of television news about bad guys who lie, cheat, steal, and break the rules in a variety of nasty ways. But I'm talking about good guys. Most of the people I know mean well. They lead purposeful lives and intend to do so until their last breath, just as these two men did.

But both found themselves beyond their limits.

Both men are senior pastors. Both are very gifted communicators and are loved and respected by the people they serve. Actually, they are held in awe. Both of them are in their fifties, leading churches with more than two thousand attending each week. Think of the pressure of that job: First of all, the pressures of preparing and delivering a message to thousands of people each week and of being very much under the spotlight. That, combined with the leadership responsibility of what is essentially a very large service enterprise, is hugely demanding.

The first person I want to describe leads a church in the western United States. He began the church himself and is well known as a writer and a speaker at leadership seminars for pastors. Not long ago, I heard him give a message describing his experience of burnout. He said he had gotten to a point where he felt like he was faking everything. He said, "I felt fried inside. I lost enthusiasm for what I was doing. The work that had been a great passion for me had become just a job. I was dragging myself through each day. I knew something was wrong, talked to a couple of friends about it, and finally sought medical help. The doctor diagnosed burnout and prescribed six months of rest—absolutely no work. It was that bad.

"I said, 'no way,' but I booked a short silent retreat in a Catholic monastery. It wasn't perfect, but it gave me enough relief to at least think deeply about what was happening to me and motivated me to cut back my work schedule significantly. I delegated responsibility for all manner of things to subordinates who did a terrific job."

The second pastor leads a large church on the opposite side of the country, and he, too, began to experience burnout. A number of people I talked to had predicted it. He was very detail-oriented and reluctant to delegate anything. He was operating a large church as if it were a small parish church, doing lots of pastoral care as well as preparing messages each week. He was a micromanager. He began to feel some physical pain, and as a result took painkillers that soon led to a deep addiction to prescription drugs. It was discovered later that multiple doctors in his congregation were prescribing strong and addictive prescription drugs, not knowing others were doing the same. In each case, he told the doctor involved not to tell his wife about it. He was like a duck that appears calm on the surface and paddles like crazy under the water just to stay afloat. The people on his board felt that something was wrong and thought that they should hire more help for him. One of them later told me, "We were treating the wrong disease in the wrong way, but how were we to know?" Things finally came to a head, and this story found its way onto the front page of a local newspaper. People were shocked. The minister was temporarily relieved of his senior pastor duties and spent six months in a treatment center and halfway house.

In the first case, the pastor is fully recovered and has restored his spiritual vitality and his passion and energy for work. He has been willing to talk about this issue with other pastors in the hope that they will be warned in time. By now, you may have recognized him as Wayne Cordeiro.

The jury is out on the second case. There's hope. This is a very intelligent man who has taken steps to restore his relationships. He still has the love of members of his congregation who worried about him beforehand. But he's not out of the woods.

I asked Dr. Larry Allums, my "personal trainer in literature," about this issue. He told me that a great deal of literature and drama turns around "the tragic flaw"—characters not admitting their limits to themselves or others. In Shakespeare, Julius Caesar is a great general but a very poor politician. King Lear was so blinded by his own self-absorption and desire to retire and take it easy that he was careless about putting his kingdom and his own future in good hands. A tragic flaw of many leaders is that they cannot recognize their limits or acknowledge their need for others as the demands of work or ministry scale up dramatically.

Leading on Empty is Wayne Cordeiro's own journey, a journey that every leader can learn from. Wise people will enlist immediately, and others may study it later, but we will all benefit from this candid description of his road to burnout. These axioms of life and leadership will be an indispensable travel guide. They may not give you quick answers, nor will they make you bulletproof.

But they will give you the ability to see further ahead . . . to recognize the dangers of the potholes along the way and also appreciate the beauty of the sunsets.

I encourage you to learn how to avoid the quagmire of burn-out, or how to escape it once you've landed there, from Wayne Cordeiro, someone who's been through it himself and has come out stronger on the other side.[1]

Preface

How do you lead when you don't feel like leading? And how do you sail through the dead waters when the wind has died down and that which was a *festival* now demands the *intentional?* When *exhilaration* turns to *perspiration?*

Like pages torn out of my journal, this book chronicles my collision with burnout and my subsequent journey to a newly defined life.

Much like C. S. Lewis's *A Grief Observed*, this book doesn't have symmetrical chapters followed by objective clinical prognoses. (When you are going through a season of burnout, nothing is symmetrical or objective.)

During this winter season, the only things I had to hold on to were the disciplines I had *already built* into my life. In the night, a sailor cannot see land, nor can he get his bearings from the coastline. He must navigate by trusting the dimly lit buoys already set in place. In the same way, when you go through dark seasons, you will be restricted by, or released to, what has already been established within your soul. This book will reveal those disciplines leaders must build *before* navigating the open seas, and if you are already storm-tossed, it will give you practical helps that will buoy up your resilience.

One daily discipline I kept throughout my journey was meeting with God each morning, and through a regimen of journaling my discoveries during those times, I would find direction and assurance. Within my spiraled *Life Journals* were chronicled the ups and downs, the stagnation and progress, the failures and triumphs of that season. I wrote in the darkest of times and the best of times. I wrote when I couldn't speak. I even wrote when I couldn't hear God.

What you have in your hands grew out of those times. It is not a textbook case study with a clear, linear progression. I have allowed some of the experiences of ambivalence to remain as a written witness of where I was and how I came back again to the sunlit land of emotional health. This treatise is not sifted, smooth, and refined, but like a tall glass of fresh-squeezed orange juice, you'll recognize some pulp. You might even encounter a few seeds.

But that doesn't take away from its value. Instead, I hope it makes it even more trustworthy and healthy.

I couldn't have made it through this time without the support of those closest to me. I want to say "Thank you" to my dear wife and family who saw me through this protracted season of transition. And to our staff at New Hope, who pulled together rather than apart.

REFLECTIONS

The end of each chapter includes a page or two of *Reflections*. These are actual experiences of the various pastors and leaders I interviewed who have worked through seasons of grief, depression, and burnout. They share unapologetically the struggles and the victories. In each *Reflection* you will find gems of wisdom that could save your life and your ministry.

Introduction

We don't forget that we are Christians. We forget that we are human, and that one oversight alone can debilitate the potential of our future.

It arrived without warning, like an uninvited guest. Decisions that were once simple now refused solution, and I found myself dodging anything that asked for my emotional input. My once stalwart faith was left fragile; I avoided whatever required my action.

It was a balmy California evening. I had gone for a jog before I was to speak at a leadership conference. I still can't recall how I got there, but I found myself sitting on a curb, weeping uncontrollably. I couldn't tell if it took place suddenly or gradually, but I knew something had broken inside. I remember lifting my trembling hands and asking out loud, "What in the world is happening to me?"

I had been *leading on empty.*

That incident on a California curb began a three-year odyssey I never could have imagined. It was a journey through a season of burnout and re-calibration that would radically change my lifestyle, my values, my goals, and even readjust my calling.

Everything I had blissfully taken for granted was about to come under brutal scrutiny.

My vision for the church was barren, and the once-alive heart that beat incessantly for others had begun to shrink. Each day that passed was taking a toll on me, but I didn't know how to stop the progression. Whatever was causing the drain was winning.

If I had been alert, I might have seen the signs before that curbside meltdown and recognized them for what they were. But for some reason, I ignored them.

One of the common anesthetics that numb us to these dark harbingers is thinking, *"It could never happen to me!"*

The signs were all around me, but I ignored them. Simple problems refused solution. Anything that necessitated emotional energy sent me in the other direction. My faith was bruised and fragile. My confident demeanor had turned pensive, and a soul that used to be an ocean of life was now a stagnant tide pool.

What had broken loose on that mild twilight run? Was it an emotional hemorrhage? If so, how would I stem the bleeding? I had no idea where to begin the triage. I had to figure out what was happening so I could somehow repair the inner damage.

But who has time for that?

My schedule determined my song and an inner conductor set the rhythm. I was simply playing the part that had been given to me, and I didn't know if I could change the score.

In this case, the road to success and the road to a nervous breakdown were one and the same.

Over the ensuing months, I would wrestle with bouts of depression, losing some rounds, but continuing the fight. With the help of a doctor, an understanding wife, a supportive church, and the strength and wisdom of God, I would survive a course of invaluable life lessons that would demand the highest tuition I have ever paid.

My love for God had not abandoned me. My marriage was stable, and the ministry seemed healthy. But I still had no idea how to confront the silent predator that was stalking me—sometimes far behind, and at other times so close I could feel its breath on my neck.

If there were a pill I could have swallowed that would have kept me from this inner collapse, I'm glad I didn't find it.

Suffering will change us, but not necessarily for the better. We have to choose that. And it was the choosing that made all the difference for me.

Chapter One
When the Needle Points to Empty

"I am weary with my groaning and have found no rest."
JEREMIAH 45:3

Not long ago I was asked to meet with two dozen of our nation's brightest and best emerging church leaders through a wonderful organization led by Bob Buford called *The Leadership Network.* The men who gathered were all around forty years old with congregations of more than three thousand members. Larry Osborne of North Coast Church and I were the supposed white-haired veterans from whom these young leaders could extract wisdom. (I hope they didn't pay much for this conference!) Nevertheless, we interacted and shared what we could.

On the second day, conference organizers asked these young leaders a question that caught many of them (myself included) off guard.

What do you fear the most?

As they each took a turn answering, tears began to flow freely, and several couldn't even finish their sentences. One admitted that he didn't know how much longer his marriage could sustain the pressure. But it was another leader's answer that grabbed my attention.

His greatest fear? "I just don't want my kids growing up hating God because of me."

Observing the lives of many of these forty-something leaders, I saw the unmistakable signs of burnout already emerging.

When the first signs of burnout appear, it's time for a break.

A mother with children in diapers doesn't have the option of leaving her babies and flying to Hawaii for a break from the late-night feedings. The stressed captain of a football team can't decide to stay home from a strategic game to watch his favorite TV sitcom. And neither can a pastor of a growing church suddenly cash in on a half-price deal for a Caribbean cruise.

> "It is in the quiet crucible of your personal, private sufferings that your noblest dreams are born and God's greatest gifts are given in compensation for what you have been through."
>
> **WINTLEY PHIPPS**

As a senior pastor, my life was book-ended with weekend services. I had developed the discipline of *image management*, but on the inside I was experiencing a slow-motion implosion.

Pastors are expected to lead even when the desire or inclination to do so is severely challenged. I knew others loved me, but living up to the expectations systemically ingrained into the fabric of who I was became the person I could not escape.

How do you lead on empty? How do you continue when you don't feel like being "on stage" anymore?

When it comes to burnout, we are in good company. . . .

SHOWDOWN AT THE O.K. CORRAL

Elijah arrived at such a moment. His dramatic story unfolds in 1 Kings 18—a showdown at the O.K. Corral, Hebrew style. The fiery-eyed backwoods prophet confronted, defeated, and utterly destroyed 850 cultic priests of Baal and Asherah bent on leaching away Israel's devotion to God. The battle ensued and Elijah prevailed.

At that point, however, the story takes an odd twist. Did the prophet really imagine that Ahab and the vixen from Sidon, Queen Jezebel, would applaud him for wiping out Samaria's state religion? But the once unflappable prophet is blindsided by the queen's rage and is suddenly scared spit-less by her venomous message:

> May the gods strike me and even kill me if by this time tomorrow I have not killed you just as you killed them.
> (1 Kings 19:2 NLT)

Elijah panicked and fled to a secluded hiding place in the wilderness. It was there, exhausted and alone, that he decided a quick death would be preferable to living the rest of his life as a fugitive.

He prayed, "Take away my life; I might as well be dead!" (1 Kings 19:4 GNT).

DEPRESSION IN THE DESERT

Moses suffered too. When he was leading the people of Israel through the desert, they started grumbling, complaining, and backbiting. The impeccable leader whose epiphany at Mount Horeb gave him the courage to take on

> "I know God will not give me anything I can't handle. I just wish He didn't trust me so much."
>
> **MOTHER TERESA**

the great pharaoh of Egypt became so exasperated and discouraged, he cried out to God: "I alone am not able to carry all this people, because it is too burdensome for me. So if You are going to deal thus with me, please kill me at once" (Numbers 11:14–15).

"Please kill me at once."

Now, that's a depressed man! He considered death preferable to continuing in his dire circumstances.

LIFE NAVIGATORS

The Bible brims with such accounts—the raw, unedited stories of men and women who have already traversed the valleys you and I are yet to experience. They have found the passageways on this journey called life, and they bid us to follow. No, they don't give us shortcuts around the obstacles we have been bid to traverse. These mentors of old are more like scouts, men and women walking the trails that lie in front of us, showing us the routes and openings—the paths we might not have seen otherwise. They post signs along the way, warning us of the pitfalls. They leave behind clutch holds in the rock where fatal choices have claimed the lives of others—those who have attempted to scale the snowcapped mountains without the aid of Sherpas.

> "The most authentic thing about us is our capacity to create, to overcome, to endure, to transform, to love, and to be greater than our suffering."
>
> **BEN OKRI**

They give us right answers before we make wrong conclusions. These life navigators have been assigned by God. They guide us through seasons in which one misstep can alter our future and diminish our legacy.

Elijah and Moses will be our guides. We have invited others as well. Jeremiah and David assure us of a way through unfamiliar and even frightening terrain. They know that much of who we will become is determined by how we negotiate those treacherous slopes. Our safe passage is only guaranteed under the condition that we follow closely.

OVERWHELMED

For over thirty years my drive for excellence propelled me. It wasn't that I was compulsive; I simply had a deep desire to do my best. I drove hard on all cylinders, not realizing that being an entrepreneur means that everything you initiate, by default you must add to your maintenance list.

It is a gift to be able to launch an inspiring vision. But unless you manage it along the way, it can turn on you, and soon the voracious appetite of the vision consumes you.

I pioneered a church, so I became its senior pastor. Starting several other churches made me the director of church planting. We went on to plant over a hundred churches, and the unspoken expectation is that when you have children, you take care of them. And you know how that goes. When the children go astray, the missing-child report indicts you as the bad parent. I would be sued three times for things done by errant staff. In addition, my desire to train emerging leaders found me the president of our newly formed Pacific Rim Bible College.

Mind you, I loved every bit of what I was doing, but all too soon I had a tiger by the tail, and I couldn't let go. It is a gift to be able to launch an inspiring vision. But unless you manage it along the way, it can turn on you, and soon the voracious appetite of the vision consumes you.

Our congregation grew to over fourteen thousand in twelve years with nine campuses linked by video downloads. I had authored eight books. The *Life Journal* I had developed required a shipping department in order to serve the wonderful churches who were partnering with us.

Now I found myself managing more than leading and dropping as many plates as I was spinning.

Then my father passed away, and within a span of two years my wife lost both of her parents. We had some struggles with our youngest, and a dear friend with whom I had begun the ministry moved on to other things. I felt like I was being swept along in a swift-moving current. My only hope was that the current would be merciful enough to push me to the side bank before I was dragged into the undertow of the rapids.

INSIDE EROSION

> Save me, O God,
> for the floodwaters are up to my neck.
> Deeper and deeper I sink into the mire;
> I can't find a foothold.
> I am in deep water,
> and the floods overwhelm me.
> (Psalm 69:1–2 NLT)

Slowly, the unwelcome symptoms began to surface. Ministry became more arduous. My daily tasks seemed unending, and e-mails began to stack up. People I deeply cared about became problems to be avoided, and deliberating about new vision no longer stirred my soul.

Although I never doubted my calling and gifting, what began as a joy that filled me now became a load that drained me. But I didn't know where I could trim. People were coming to Christ and lives were being changed. How could this all be wrong?

Decisions—even small ones—seemed to paralyze me. Gradually my creativity began to flag and I found it easier to imitate rather than innovate. I was backing away from the very things that used to challenge and invigorate me.

CURBSIDE BREAKDOWN

Finally it came to a head while I was out on a run on that balmy California evening. One minute I was jogging along on the sidewalk, and the next minute I was sitting on the curb, sobbing uncontrollably. I couldn't stop, and I didn't have a clue what was happening to me.

Somehow I made it through the speaking engagement that night and limped home to Hawaii. Back home again, my situation seemed to go from bad to worse. I began developing physical symptoms: erratic heartbeat, difficulty in breathing, insomnia.

New fears began to mushroom. Remembering that my father had passed away from heart disease and high blood pressure, I began wondering if that was to be my fate as well. I might be next in line for a genetic baton pass.

> "Worry is a cycle of inefficient thoughts whirling around a center of fear."
>
> **CORRIE TEN BOOM**

Fearing the worst, I made a visit to a cardiologist, who ran me through the usual battery of tests: electrocardiogram, stress test, echocardiogram, everything short of the invasive angiogram. All I could think about was whether or not I had enough money to retire. I was fifty-two years old, but I was already thinking about pulling my plane into the hangar.

For over thirty years I had invested my life in Christian ministry—twenty of those years as a senior pastor in Hawaii. Along the way, I had segued from one ministry to another, adding more and more responsibilities—without pauses. But now I wasn't sure I could keep going.

COMING TO GRIPS

A few months later while guest teaching at a seminary, I struck up a casual conversation with a pastor from Canada. We began talking about the diminishing shelf life of pastors and leaders: how those whose vocation is all about *giving* out are *wearing* out.

"I was there," he reflected. "I was ready to pull the plug, but just at that time I graciously received an offer to enroll in this degree program through a full scholarship. It was a lifesaver for me. I had come to a point where I would either drop out of ministry or destroy the one I was in."

> ### Those whose vocation is all about *giving* out are *wearing* out.

Then he said, almost in passing, "I have found that after about twenty years, pastors of growing churches need to take a sabbatical because, like me, their serotonin levels are depleted."

Serotonin?

As I walked away from that conversation, something told me I had just experienced a divine appointment. It was as though this Canadian pastor had been reading my e-mail. But the learning session wasn't over; it would simply continue at another location.

Two weeks later, I was speaking at another leadership conference in Los Angeles. Following one of my teaching sessions, I was privileged to get a visit from a longtime friend who pastored at a nearby church. We hadn't been in contact for some years, so it was a joyful surprise for me to see him and spend a little time with him.

In our brief conversation, I asked him how his ministry was going. His answer set me back on my heels.

"I'm no longer in the ministry, Wayne."

My friend went on to say that he didn't know what he should do next in life. He only knew he had to quit the pastorate. For the past couple of years, he told me, he had found himself burned-out on the inside, and he could no longer keep up the pace. He had simply concluded that the best thing for his health and for his church was to resign.

"How long had you been a pastor?" I asked.

"A little over twenty years," he told me.

There it was again. *Twenty years.* I was beginning to catch the hint.

I have never experienced a theophany, where Christ appears physically to a person, but this would be as close as it gets.

RECOGNIZING THE PROBLEM

When I got back to Hawaii, I immediately made an appointment with a Christian psychologist, who confirmed my suspicions. "You have depleted your system," he said. "Your serotonin levels are completely exhausted."

There was that word again that I didn't understand the first time around. He went on to explain.

"Serotonin is a chemical like an endorphin. It's a natural, feel-good hormone. It replenishes during times of rest and then fuels you while you're working. If, however, you continue to drive yourself without replenishing, your store of serotonin will be depleted. As a substitute, your body will be forced to replace the serotonin with *adrenaline*.

"The problem is that adrenaline is designed for emergency use only. It's like those doors in a restaurant that when opened cause an alarm to sound. Our problem, though, is that we use

> "Adrenaline arousal can be compared to revving up a car engine, then leaving it to idle at high speed."
>
> **DR. ARCHIBALD D. HART,** *THE HIDDEN LINK BETWEEN ADRENALINE AND STRESS*

these pathways designed for emergency only, but no alarm sounds. Not at first, anyway.

"Should you continue to run on adrenaline, it will destroy your system. You will burn out sooner on the inside than you're able to see on the outside. The fuel of adrenaline that keeps your engines running in the beginning will turn on you and destroy you in the end."

Over the next two hours we spoke about the symptoms and the remedies. I asked, "What do I need to do?"

> **The only way to finish strong will be to first replenish your system. If you don't, prepare for a crash.**

He explained, "Serotonin can get depleted when you don't live with a cadence that allows it to be replenished. This happens in all types of people, but it is most obvious in Type A leaders and those who live with an overload of expectations. Depression takes the place of initiative; your indecision and anxiety increases. You begin to feel a greater need for aloneness and isolation. This isn't a sign of sinfulness or abnormality. At this point, however, a break from your ministry would allow those chemistry levels to return to normal."

> "Sorrow comes to all. . . . Perfect relief is not possible, except with time. You cannot now realize that you will ever feel better and yet you are sure to be happy again."
>
> **ABRAHAM LINCOLN**

"Can't you just give me a pill and make all of this disappear?" I asked, tongue-in-cheek.

I will never forget what he said next. This would become the focus of my next three years.

"I could, but it would only mask the real problem. You need to recharge, then reflect on what the trigger points were, and finally, restructure the way you're living."

He continued, "But the first step is to recharge. And that takes time."

"How much time?"

"Six months to a year."

"Six months to a year?" I gasped. "There is no way I can do that! Maybe six *weeks*, but not six *months*. Why so long?"

"Your system has to recharge, but it requires a trickle charge, one that restores you with a sustained low-amperage. There is no quick return on this one. If you do this right, you may return to the level of ministry you had in the beginning. But honestly," he continued, "most never return to the level of performance they had before the burnout. If you can't take a year, take as long as you can. Any amount is better than nothing. The only way to finish strong will be to first replenish your system. If you don't, prepare for a crash."

Well, I had come close enough to those crash points that I knew he meant what he said. The pace was not something I could sustain for much longer. I had to restructure the way I lived. My RPMs were at redline, but I didn't know how to shift gears.

THE JOURNEY BEGINS

What I would go through over the following three years was a season of epic proportions. As Charles Dickens wrote in *A Tale of Two Cities*, "It was the best of times; it was the worst of times." Worst, because I would suffer setbacks, struggles, depression, and imbalance. Although I managed to hold it all together during this time, I knew I would pay a high price for maintaining such a pace.

> "How few there are who have courage enough to own their faults, or resolution enough to mend them."
>
> **BENJAMIN FRANKLIN**

Yet it would be the best of times too.

I would learn more about myself than at any other time in my life. The habits I developed early on—my self-disciplines, unrelenting work ethic, and the drive for excellence—would cloak my inner struggles and anesthetize the pain.

GETTING OFF THE WAVE

You can usually spot an amateur in just a few seconds.

Hawaii is one of the great surfing capitals of the world. Frequently out of breath, the newbies on the waves fight the ocean rhythms instead of dancing with them. They work harder than necessary to catch a swell, and finally on, their balance betrays them and they find themselves gasping for air in the foam of the white water. Then they spar with the waves for another half hour only to repeat act one.

> **But one of the true marks of a veteran is not how he catches a wave, but whether he knows when and how to get *off* the wave.**

Veteran surfers, on the other hand, possess an uncanny sense of the ocean's currents and how waves behave. Their intuition tells them which ones to catch and which ones to let pass. They seem to discern which waves will carry them in and which waves will do them in!

But one of the true marks of a veteran is not how he catches a wave, but whether he knows when and how to get *off* the wave.

Not long ago, I was surfing my canoe in a favorite spot in front of Diamond Head, Hawaii's most photographed landmark. Seeing a monster wave building, I began paddling to gain speed. I needed to catch this one!

And I caught it all right.

The towering wave picked me—and my canoe—up, and even though I stopped paddling, it had us both in its jaws. With my hair flying and wind in my face, I was being propelled without control toward the shore. The sheer velocity of the wave beneath my canoe left me wondering whether I had really made the best choice, but it was too late to reconsider. Streaking landward down the face of this watery mountain, I noticed other surfers straddling their boards, observing me go by with intense curiosity. No one attempted to join me in my new adventure.

That was not a good sign.

The wave continued to build until I was perpendicular to the blue ocean that was receding farther and farther beneath me. That was right before I noticed the bed of coral. The last thing I remember thinking before the lights went out was, *"How do I get off this wave?"*

When I finally came up for air, the leash that tethered me to my canoe had been ripped off my leg. I had apparently survived the crash, but my carbon fiber canoe was torn wide open with subsequent waves scraping it along the reef toward shore. Even after several repairs, it has never been the same. (I recently sold it for far less than what I paid for it.)

LESSONS FROM THE REEFS

Life can sometimes pick you up like that, and it will be thrilling for a while. Ministry, business, and life itself can dupe you into thinking the ride will last forever and that there are no coral heads in your future . . . just soft sand, beach umbrellas, and fairy dust.

> "When you're finished changing, you're finished."
>
> **BENJAMIN FRANKLIN**

The trick is to know when to get off the wave. But that doesn't come easily. You need to be willing to give up the thrill of speed and advance for safety and longevity. For me, that didn't sound like a good trade.

God is not cruel, but He is not lenient. He is true; He is not safe. He is unchanging; therefore we must change. We must learn in order to succeed. Our failures do not influence our grades, but our unwillingness to learn from them does.

I knew I had to get outside help for this journey that I was about to embark on. But for now, I had to motor on, even though I knew I was . . .

Leading on empty.

———

Reflections

I had been on a mission trip. I took an overnight flight home, and when I arrived, someone took me straight to church. I preached and then had a leadership meeting. I went home and went to sleep. Two hours later I awoke in extreme panic. I had chest pains and my head felt like it was being crushed. I couldn't tell the difference between boiling water and cold water in the shower. I was conscious that I was in severe stress mode. The panic attack lasted twenty-four hours a day for the next three months, and then slowly decreased over the next six months. It took me nine months to get back into full-time work. I realized that for nearly ten years I had trained my body to ignore all the physical warnings. When I was tired, I wouldn't sleep. When I was ill, I wouldn't stop.

But now I was so sick I couldn't push on. In the first three months the intensity was so bad I contemplated ending my life. I immediately sought help.

For me to survive I had to do everything possible to get well. That meant addressing body, soul, and spirit. There was no point in asking why this had happened. I knew why. Instead, I asked myself what I must do to get better.

—*A PASTOR FROM THE WEST COAST*

Chapter Two
Forced to Failure

"Woe is me, for I am undone!"
Isaiah 6:5 NKJV

Over the years of shepherding people, I found that giving myself permission to heal came hard. I'm not sure what it was—maybe my background of being raised by a strict military father—but I always felt guilty when I took a break.

But now . . . I had to find permission to heal.

I had to find permission to heal.

A slightly skewed view of life may be undetectable and benign in the beginning, but it will become increasingly corrosive later on. There are things built into the psyches of those of us bent on making our lives count for eternity that can later cause diminishing returns.

Zeal and good intentions can fuel us in the beginning, but they won't last in the long haul. All of those good intentions and high self-expectations can eventually eat full-time shepherds alive when our expectations are inevitably disappointed. We're reduced to the lower spectrums of the food chain, and we become the prey rather than the hunter.

AGAINST ALL ODDS

> "If a man does not keep pace with his companions, perhaps it is because he hears a different drummer. Let him step to the music which he hears, however measured or far away."
>
> **HENRY DAVID THOREAU**

I hadn't realized that as a pastor I was involved in a vocation that had a dismal track record. It might be the pressures involved, or it could be the high expectations. But in either case, I found that a large number of those in pastoral ministry did not finish well.

In H. B. London Jr.'s great work *Pastors at Greater Risk*, we find these startling statistics:[1]

- 80 percent believe that pastoral ministry affects their families negatively.

- 33 percent say that being in ministry is an outright hazard to their family.

- 75 percent report they've had a significant stress-related crisis at least once in their ministry.

- 50 percent feel unable to meet the needs of the job.

- 90 percent feel they're inadequately trained to cope with ministry demands.

- 25 percent of pastors' wives see their husband's work schedule as a source of conflict.

- Those in ministry are equally likely to have their marriage end in divorce as general church members.

- The clergy has the second highest divorce rate among all professions.

- 80 percent of pastors say they have insufficient time with their spouse.

- 56 percent of pastors' wives say that they have no close friends.

- 45 percent of pastors' wives say the greatest danger to them and their family is physical, emotional, mental, and spiritual burnout.

- 52 percent of pastors say they and their spouses believe that being in pastoral ministry is hazardous to their family's well-being and health.

- 45.5 percent of pastors say that they've experienced depression or burnout to the extent that they needed to take a leave of absence from ministry.

- 70 percent do not have someone they consider a close friend.

Yes, those are statistics, and it's easy for us to shrug off a list of numbers. But it's a different story when instead of reading statistics, you find yourself on the verge of becoming one. Thinking the symptoms would disappear after a couple of days at the beach, I continued the pace, not realizing the tsunami that was building. I had to come to grips with the condition of my soul.

> "To keep a lamp burning we have to keep putting oil in it."
>
> **MOTHER TERESA**

GREAT EXPECTATIONS

To finish strong, you must learn to rejuvenate your spirit early in your ministry. Most of the people in our churches have no idea how demanding ministry can be or even how demanding *they* can be. When younger pastors begin in ministry, they think: *This feels right. People need me; they value me; I'm serving God; I'm right where I need to be.*

But as the years go by, always being on call can wear you down. A crisis is always just one phone call away, and when I was younger, it made me feel needed and valuable. But now it made me feel imprisoned.

If I am taking a break or on vacation within the state, people have no problem calling me back for a funeral or a newly surfaced marriage crisis. It's a "Catch-22." If I do not return, I may be accused of not caring. It seems impersonal and insensitive to reply, "I'm sorry, I'm not able to come. I'm on vacation. I've asked the assistant pastor to take care of things in my absence. Could you call him?" Often I have been reluctant to refuse for fear that if word gets out that I didn't come back, people will be disgruntled. On the other hand, if I do go back, my family suffers along with my own emotional health.

> "To do great work a man must be very idle as well as very industrious."
>
> **SAMUEL BUTLER**

Congregants expect pastors to preach the finest sermons in town, and when one weekend's message is completed, it's time to start work on the next one. One pastor told me it's like giving birth on Sunday; then on Monday you find out you're pregnant again!

After thirty years of this weekly pattern, the pressure of coming up with one more inspirational sermon had me worn down, but I couldn't stop the train. I was expected to lead on empty.

It was no one's fault. That's just how we're wired, and if we don't rewire things, we burn out the circuit board. I was fixing everybody's problems except my own, and I needed time to replenish my spirit.

THE WALL

Sooner or later every long-distance runner encounters the wall. Regardless of how well-trained the athlete, he will meet it one day, and he will meet it head on.

The wall is the term for the invisible moment at about the twenty-mile mark of a marathon when the body is wracked with fatigue and an apparently insurmountable physiological barrier stops the runner in his tracks.

The marathon is a 26.2-mile footrace. I have run four of them and the wall greeted me all four times. It happens when an athlete's glycogen reserves are depleted. At this point, having run out of fuel, the body makes a shift and starts to tap into its fat reserves as a fuel source.

While veteran long-distance runners may feel temporarily out of steam, the more inexperienced runners will suffer from additional physiological problems, including muscle cramps from lactic acid buildup and dehydration.

> "When a man is pushed, tormented, defeated, he has a chance to learn something."
>
> **RALPH WALDO EMERSON**

Those who train for marathons prepare their bodies by forcing them to failure. Weight lifters and body builders do the same thing. Marathoners educate their bodies to accept the sudden change from glycogen to fat by doing a number of long training runs that endure through this fuel change zone. The body then adapts to the switch from the main to auxiliary fuel supply, so that hitting the wall will be less of a shock.

Merely identifying something is not the same as getting it addressed and resolved.

Once the runner is through the wall, the worst is over, and providing there are no other ill effects, such as blisters or cramps, the finish line should be inevitable.

IDENTIFYING IS NOT RESOLVING

I met with my counselor several more times until I understood what was going on in my emotional state, but merely identifying something is not the same as getting it addressed and resolved. It's the classic scenario of rearranging deck chairs on the *Titanic*.

After thirty years of a marathon ministry, I hit the wall—and I had no idea how to switch to another fuel system. What gives you thrust in the beginning often abandons you at the twenty-mile marker.

Every runner will hit the wall . . . but for me, the wall hit back.

One afternoon I was driving home from the office and suspected I was having a heart attack. I felt my left arm go numb and struggled to catch my breath. Pulling over to the side of the road, I called my doctor on my cell. After I explained the symptoms and answered a few of his questions, he concluded, "Wayne, you're not having a heart attack. You're experiencing an *anxiety* attack. But if you keep this pace up, you *will* have a heart attack . . . soon! You either take a break, or I can give you some medication."

> **I hit the wall. I needed a new fuel and a restructured life.**

I knew I couldn't put it off any longer. The wave had grown bigger than I had ever imagined and was pushing me toward a hard landing on an unforgiving reef. A break or medication—it was my choice.

MEDICATION OR MONASTERY

Some months prior, a friend had remarked how therapeutic it had been for him to spend time at a California coastal retreat center run by Catholic monks. The quietness and solitude, he had remarked, had renewed and refreshed his soul.

I needed God to quiet every voice but His own.

Checking into a monastery seemed a little drastic, but I knew I had to do something. So I called my friend for the address and embarked on my journey to the coast of California. I would spend a week with the monks, needing God to quiet every voice but His own.

Catholic monks who had taken a vow of silence manned the center deep in the coastal mountains. When I arrived, I quickly discovered what the vow of silence entailed. Walking into the office, I was greeted by a bare notice: "Your cabin awaits your arrival. Please proceed down the lane to Cabin 4."

That was it. No greeter. No check-in clerk. No bell-boys. Just a note with thirteen words, and even those were read with a whisper. I checked into my humble surroundings and unpacked. I retired early but couldn't sleep.

The following morning, at precisely four o'clock, I discovered the chapel bell tolled for me. Its clappered voice greeted monks and pilgrims alike with thirty soundings. Yes, I counted them. I also found that the only time these hooded monks used their voices was at

> "Loneliness is the poverty of self; solitude is the richness of self."
>
> **MAY SARTON**

five o'clock as they gathered for morning prayers. Bleary-eyed, I entered the chapel to the acoustic sounds of a cappella monks singing the Psalms in Gregorian chant. The purity of simple harmonies brushed the dimly lit chapel with a soft radiance that actually felt warm. The beauty of the deep, resonant voices softly reminded me that God had begun His work.

Silence and solitude can renew and replenish a soul in drought, and it refreshed me. I returned to my silent cabin to have my devotions, but for a boy from the city with encrusted habits, silence can have its limits. I found that in this monastic retreat there were no Internet hookups, no cell phones, and—worst of all—*no coffee*. The placid retreat started to feel more like a penal colony. After all, how could I do devotions without coffee and a muffin?

Silence and solitude can renew and replenish a soul in drought.

The second day my system began to shut down. Dropping adrenaline is like coming off heroin. There are obvious withdrawals, and my body started cramping. My journal entry that morning read, "I have never had this much pain in my life. I am not sure what is happening, but I need to ride this one out." I felt Isaiah's pain when he wrote, "Woe is me, for I am undone!" (6:5 NKJV). I remember crying out to God in the night as sleep once again eluded me.

During those days at the monastery, I found myself separated from just about every one of the bonding agents that had held me together through the years: my family, my schedule, the pastoral office hours, the meetings, the speaking, and even my regimen of exercise. I felt unnecessary, unneeded, and undone. I felt swept away.

Maybe it was time for a new endeavor, a different direction, a fresh career. My hunger for what I was doing had subsided, and I was sure God was giving me a new assignment. Maybe it was to change careers. Could it be that I wasn't cut out for the ministry after all?

My reasoning capabilities were clouded and reevaluation was premature. I just needed time to heal without running myself through a self-inflicted battery of tests. I needed to do the most urgent thing of all . . . rest. I needed every voice to be stilled, even my own. But even that came hard. As a pastor, I was pre-programmed to fix things that were broken, but this one had me stumped.

So the only thing that I kept steady was my daily time at His feet. And it would be here that my answers, and my strength, would eventually appear.

> **It would be here that my answers, and my strength, would eventually appear. It was in my daily devotions that the prophet Jeremiah saved my life.**

Wisdom and understanding are not built in a day; however they are built *daily*. And it was on one of those days in my devotions that the prophet Jeremiah saved my life.

PROPHETIC RESCUE

I was lost at sea. I was treading water, not knowing how long I could last. Sometimes I felt myself in the grip of panic, and at other times I felt nothing but total exhaustion.

All I was certain of was that I was sinking. That's when Jeremiah threw me a plank. Not a life raft, mind you, just a plank. But it was enough to keep me afloat until help arrived.

"The way to see by faith is to shut the eye of reason."

BENJAMIN FRANKLIN

I had been spending time with Jeremiah, when I began to notice an eerie similarity between my current experience and his. As I read the prophet's journal of rejection, disappointment, and emotional pain, it began to dawn on me that I wasn't alone in this. In fact, I was experiencing only a fraction of what he had endured.

"I don't care," I mumbled. "I think I'm through. I'd like to do something else. I've paid my dues. I've put in my time. Now it's someone else's turn."

My musings continued into the seventeenth chapter of Jeremiah, when he finally spoke in a way I could understand. After several hours of moaning about throwing in the towel, I heard the embattled prophet speak as clearly as I have ever heard anyone speak. He chastised me as only a friend could, leaving not a wound but a conviction.

"If you want to quit, then quit! Don't be so wishy-washy. If you want to drop out, drop out. Quit whining."

Then looking skyward, speaking to the One who enlisted him in the first place, he said with an audible sigh: "But as for me, I have not hurried away from being a shepherd after You" (Jeremiah 17:16).

That was the plank. That was what kept me alive and gave me hope again. Then he turned to me as if to say, "Isn't it time we took a walk?"

It was the mild rebuke of one friend to another. "You can call it quits if you want to, but as for me? I wouldn't be so quick."

> "Nobody ever outgrows Scripture; the Book widens and deepens with our years."
>
> **CHARLES H. SPURGEON**

It was what I needed. Not the affirmation I was looking for, perhaps, but whatever it was, it saved my ministry. I didn't receive an answer, but I gained the *resolve necessary to press forward.*

Your future will oftentimes be held "in trust" within the simplicity of a daily walk with God. The discovery of hidden potential will be gently pressed within the pages of His Word. Even though the way before you may be foggy or dim, the path beneath you will be illuminated by a warm and steady light. But without the walk, without the light, tomorrow can seem darker than we'd ever imagined it could be.

Isn't it time we took a walk together? Join me.

_____

Reflections

I began to sense my burnout before anyone else did. I kept telling the people around me that I needed to stop. But they told me, "We're in this building program; we need you." People wanted me to make decisions, but I couldn't. I vacillated. I avoided confrontation. I got to the point that I didn't want to come into the office. But when the tears wouldn't stop flowing for me, they realized that I needed a break.

Some thought that something sinful had happened in my life. But I couldn't deal with everyone's thoughts then. I had to deal with me. It was the lousiest time in my life, but when I look back on it I wouldn't want to miss the lessons that I learned along the way.

I was angry with God that He had not heard my prayers. I was filled with despair that I wasn't getting a lot of answers. I kept wondering why I had to deal with the problems I was facing at church. Every day I was grappling with just who God is. I was closing down. My theology said that if I prayed and fasted all would come together.

I tried to push through the early stages of burnout. I just made myself get up and get going. I'd tell myself, "I can do this." I was bewildered. "Where is this coming from?" I asked myself over and over again.

I took one thing at a time. First I focused on getting my mind under control. Then I worked on renewing my spirit, and then finally I worked on my body.

—Business leader from the Northwest

Chapter Three
Power Perfected in Weakness

"And He has said to me, 'My grace is sufficient for you, for power is perfected in weakness.'. . . Therefore I am well content with weaknesses, with insults, with distresses, with persecutions, with difficulties, for Christ's sake; for when I am weak, then I am strong."

2 CORINTHIANS 12:9–10

"It could never happen to me."

Those were the famous last words just before it happened to me. But often burnout doesn't arrive alone. One unlikely twin (for me) that accompanied my season of burnout was depression. It bewildered me. I am normally gregarious, and loving people comes easily for

"There in those caves, drowned in the sorrow of his song and in the song of his sorrow, David became the greatest hymn writer and the greatest comforter of broken hearts this world shall ever know."

GENE EDWARDS,
A TALE OF THREE KINGS

me, so when I was blindsided by ambivalence and de-motivation, I was befuddled.

Permit me to turn aside for the next two chapters to a malicious cousin that often attends burnout: *depression*. Traveling partners, they are the Bonnie and Clydes of life, setting you back months and robbing you of years. But they don't just *happen* upon you at random. There are several triggers that exacerbate the problem and bring it to a boiling point. No one is immune from the slow grip of depression when they are wrestling through a season of burnout. It is an uninvited guest that you endure, then with God's help, resolve. More serious levels of depression that are accompanied by thoughts of suicide will require immediate attention, but mine were rather a constant visitation of a sense of exasperation and inner surrender.

> "We shall draw from the heart of suffering itself the means of inspiration and survival."
>
> **WINSTON CHURCHILL**

Depression haunts you with feelings of worthlessness and clouds your hope. It attacks your faith and it smothers your future. Bouts of crying, a general decrease of pleasure in life, and a lessened energy follow you like shadows increasing into dark days and long nights. It has complexities that are difficult to unravel and physical, emotional, and spiritual symptoms.

Depression is no respecter of persons. The silent "terrorist" attacks those outside of the church as well as those within. Those outside, however, seem better able to accept its reality and find ways to cope. After all, shouldn't Christians be immune from these things? Shouldn't followers of Christ be constantly filled with the joy of the Lord?

UNTOUCHABLES IN THE KINGDOM

Sadly, more times than not those stricken with depression are seen as emotional lepers, the walking wounded. Some view depression as deserved justice for unconfessed sin or unresolved contentions.

All too often a Christian struggling with burnout and depression will encounter snippets of advice like these from well-meaning counselors:

- "Confess your guilt."

- "Pray more."

- "Find a new church."

- "Read this self-help book."

- "You just need more faith."

- "Read your Bible more."

> "The ultimate measure of a man is not where he stands in moments of comfort and convenience, but where he stands at times of challenge and controversy."
>
> **MARTIN LUTHER KING JR.**

Sound like Job's comforters? In an article titled "Why Am I So Depressed?" Brenda Poinsett speaks of the interrogation she experienced when she mentioned her own depression: "Were you a believer at the time?" "Were you walking with the Lord?" "Were you reading the Bible and praying?"

She says, "When I answer yes to these questions, I can almost hear another question forming in the silence that follows: 'How could a faithful, growing believer get depressed?'" She continues, "This question reveals a common, unspoken, and inaccurate assumption: Christians are not supposed to struggle with depression."[1]

But we have many examples from Scripture of men and women of God struggling with depression. Isaiah called it being "undone." Jeremiah said he wished he'd never been born. Moses asked God to blot him out of the Book of Life, and Jonah said that for him, death was better than life. Job's struggles are a continuing saga throughout the book that bears his name. Even Jesus, entering into a time of intense prayer in the garden of Gethsemane, was in "great despair."

DEPRESSED SAINTS

Down through the centuries, many of God's choicest saints have wrestled with a tenacious, life-sapping melancholy and depression in seasons of their lives.

Mother Teresa (1910–1997)

The late Mother Teresa has been a heroine of mine for years. Her books have tutored me in many ways, yet she dealt with feelings of being abandoned by God. In personal correspondence, she wrote: "I am told God loves me—and yet the reality of darkness and coldness and emptiness is so great that nothing touches my soul."[2]

> "I am told God loves me—and yet the reality of darkness and coldness and emptiness is so great that nothing touches my soul."
>
> **MOTHER TERESA**

I understand her feelings of loneliness. She continued: "I feel just that terrible pain of loss, of God not wanting me, of God not being God, of God not really existing." Yet even though she struggled until the end of her life, she delivered hope to thousands of the poorest of the poor in Calcutta, India.

William Cowper (1731–1800)

William Cowper was the son of a clergyman. His mother, Anne, died when he was not yet six years old, so in his earlier years, he was sent to a private boarding school where he was terrorized and belittled by hateful classmates.

He was later educated at Westminster. During the course of his service there, he became very anxious and distressed, and was eventually hospitalized with depression at St. Albans. Yet he pressed through to bring forth hymns that have filled countless churches with the music of faith and hope.[3]

In July 1764, while sitting in his garden, he read Romans 3: 24–25: "Being justified as a gift by His grace through the redemption which is in Christ Jesus . . . This was to demonstrate His righteousness, because in the forbearance of God He passed over the sins previously committed."

He related, "Immediately I received strength to believe and the full beams of the Son of Righteousness shone upon me. I saw the sufficiency of the atonement that Christ had made: my pardon in His blood, the fullness and completeness of my justification. In a moment I believed and received the Gospel."[4]

> "I seem forsaken and alone, I hear the lion roar; and every door is shut but one, and that is Mercy's door."
>
> **WILLIAM COWPER**

Cowper was a close friend of John Newton, the author of the hymn "Amazing Grace." Together they published what became known as the Olney Hymns. Cowper is best known for these lines from "Light Shining Out of Darkness":

> God moves in a mysterious way,
> His wonders to perform;
> He plants His footsteps in the sea,
> And rides upon the storm.
>
> Deep in unfathomable mines
> Of never-failing skill
> He treasures up his bright designs
> And works His sovereign will.

Charles Haddon Spurgeon (1834–1892)

Charles Haddon Spurgeon was one of the greatest preachers of all time, beloved for his outstanding ability to communicate God's Word, his sparkling wit, and quick humor. Yet this man who addressed crowds of up to twenty thousand people suffered a lifetime battle with depression. "My success," he once wrote, "appalled me; and the thought of the career which it seemed to open up, so far from elating me, cast me into the lowest depth, out of which I uttered my misery."[5]

> "The ministry is a matter which wears the brain and strains the heart, and drains out the life of a man if he attends to it as he should."
>
> **CHARLES H. SPURGEON**

Spurgeon felt great anxiety from the "awesome responsibility of being accountable to God for the souls of so many." He remarked in 1883: "I have preached the gospel now these thirty years and more, and . . . often, in coming down to this pulpit, have I felt my knees knock together, not that I am afraid of any one of my hearers, but I am thinking of that account which I must render to God, whether I speak his Word faithfully or not."[6]

During his early years in London, he was often the object of intense slander, ridicule, and contempt. He wrestled between "rejoicing in such persecution and being utterly crushed by it." In 1857, he struggled: "Down on my knees have I often fallen, with the hot sweat rising from my brow under some fresh slander poured upon me; in an agony of grief my heart has been well-nigh broken. . . . This thing I hope I can say from my heart: If to be made as the mire of the streets again, if to be the laughingstock of fools and the song of the drunkard once more will make me more serviceable to my Master, and more useful to his cause, I will prefer it to all this multitude, or to all the applause that man could give."[7]

Spurgeon viewed his depression as a means of equipping him to minister more effectively: "I would go into the deeps a hundred times to cheer a downcast spirit. It is good for me to have been afflicted, that I might know how to speak a word in season to one that is weary."[8]

Abraham Lincoln (1809–1865)

Abraham Lincoln, whose "House Divided Against Itself" speech helped win him the presidency, knew all too well in his own life the awful agony of doubt and depression. Early in his life he wrote, "I am now the most miserable man living. If what I feel were equally distributed to the whole human family, there would not be one cheerful face on the earth. Whether I shall ever be better I can not tell; I awfully forebode I shall not. To remain as I am is impossible; I must die or be better, it appears to me."[9]

> "I am now the most miserable man living. . . . Whether I shall ever be better, I cannot tell. I awfully forebode I shall not."
>
> **ABRAHAM LINCOLN,** LETTER TO JOHN T. STUART, JANUARY 23, 1841[9]

Martin Luther King Jr. (1929–1968)

A champion of the civil rights movement, Martin Luther King Jr.'s legacy will always be synonymous with racial equality and social change. His brief life, however, was marked with turbulence and struggle—not only heroic efforts, but also desperate stretches of depression that sometimes alarmed his closest colleagues and friends. Because of his deep descents into the doldrums, he was asked to see a psychiatrist by one of his top aides. His sleeping pills no longer effective, he became preoccupied with death.

> "We must accept finite disappointment, but never lose infinite hope."
>
> **MARTIN LUTHER KING JR.**

Henri Nouwen (1932–1996)

Henri Nouwen was a Dutch Catholic priest and author of forty books. He spent some time at the L'Arche community in France for the mentally handicapped. This led him to accept the position of pastor for Daybreak, the L'Arche community in Toronto, in 1986. His works include *The Inner Voice of Love*, *The Return of the Prodigal Son*, *Adam*, *Compassion*, and *Life of the Beloved*.

Nouwen had serious bouts of clinical depression, and one of the major ongoing themes in his works involved his struggle to reconcile his depression with his Christian faith.

"It is important to become aware that at every moment of our life we have an opportunity to choose joy. . . . It is in the choice that our true freedom lies, and that freedom is, in the final analysis, the freedom to love."

HENRI NOUWEN

These comrades would often walk through the valley of the shadow of death. Their worlds crumbled around them, and the skies remained dark for months at a time. Yet even though their loneliness was acute and real, God never left them.

These saints dealt with some of the issues in their lives that you and I do—some of which can lead to depression.

CAUSES OF DEPRESSION

In earlier days of medicine, surgery was something like a death sentence. The number of patients who did not survive surgical procedures perplexed doctors. Patient after patient died from "unknown causes." The surgeons would operate on one patient, walk to the next one, continue their surgical procedures, and then move on to a third. Unwittingly, they were transferring bacteria from one patient to the next. But with the development of germ theory by Louis Pasteur, medical professionals began to discover the infinitesimal harbingers of infection. Armed with this new knowledge, physicians could combat the mysterious courier of diseases. Medicine took a major stride forward.

Likewise, the more knowledge you have about the causes and symptoms of burnout and depression, the better equipped you will be to meet and resolve these situations.

Let's take a look at where depression often begins. Several triggers can unleash the landslide of depression. Every one of us fallen human beings is susceptible to dismay and exasperation. Like a powerful undertow, life has its own entropy, a constant tide that pulls ever so gently but ever so consistently. As time lapses and our defenses get weary, we can be caught in a tidal wave of emotions with neurochemical reactions. Here are a few common triggers:

> "We turn to God for help when our foundations are shaking, only to learn that it is God who is shaking them."
>
> **CHARLES C. WEST**

Long-Term Stress

Long-term stress is a predecessor to depression. The constant expectation to come up with yet another inspiring message wears you out. It depletes your emotional system, reducing your ability to stay balanced. Long-term stress is not detectable in the beginning. It is well disguised by growing success, financial prosperity, or people's accolades. The numbing effect keeps you pressing forward, leading on empty, until the bottom falls out. Then success is no longer your goal. Healing is.

Long-term stress depletes the normal fuel produced biochemically by hormones and secreted into the brain and nervous system. These endorphins and other peptides produce an analgesic effect. Once these serotonins are exhausted, adrenaline has to be produced to take their place. Soon an addiction to adrenaline puts a demand on your body for greater amounts. Adrenaline, also known as epinephrine, is secreted in increasing rates, and your body becomes dependent on this powerful chemical to meet deadlines, get reports ready, and rise to the expectations of others—or your own.

Adrenaline addiction is an emotional suicide that will slowly progress and may be difficult to detect. If not recognized, stress will precede burnout, and burnout is often accompanied by a super-sized helping of depression.

> **Long-term stress depletes the normal fuel produced biochemically by hormones and secreted into the brain and nervous system.**

When the mind is put under the constant stress of deadlines, anxiety results and throws the body into crisis mode. Blood pressure increases, heart rates rise, and cholesterol counts swell. This accelerated wear and tear results in ulcers, anxiety attacks, and heart disease.

You might feel important and necessary for the moment, but that fleeting sense of self-importance has a price you will not be able to afford.

The emotional debt may demand everything you have, and that which once thrilled you now stands as your accuser.

Great Loss

David felt it, along with a large band of his rugged warriors. The Bible tells us that "when David and his men came to the city, behold, it was burned with fire, and their wives and their sons and their daughters had been taken captive. Then David and the people who were with him lifted their voices and wept until there was no strength in them to weep" (1 Samuel 30:3–4).

> "God is unchanging in His love. He loves you. He has a plan for your life. . . . God is still sovereign; He's still on the throne."
>
> **BILLY GRAHAM**

Ever feel that way? The death of a loved one, a ministry failure, a church split, job loss, or a divorce can trigger depression, especially when your resilience is low and you don't feel ready for a quick return to business as usual.

All too often well-meaning people will offer shallow remedies that exacerbate the pain: "Get over it!" "Just look forward." "Toughen up." "God is able!" "Let's move on."

These comments, however well-intended, are no help at all. We may be sons and daughters of God in Christ, but we are also flesh-and-blood human beings. Even God keeps that in mind, as the psalm reminds us: "For he knows how we are formed, he remembers that we are dust" (Psalm 103:14 NIV). Furthermore, there is no time limit to the grieving process. An important part of the journey to healing is allowing oneself to experience and accept all the feelings that roll like waves over our soul.

Unresolved Problems

The psalmist knew that until something could be resolved, his soul would be troubled.

> My tears have been my food day and night, while they say to me all day long, "Where is your God?" . . . I used to go along with the throng and lead them in procession to the house of God, with the voice of joy and thanksgiving, a multitude keeping festival. Why are you in despair, O my soul? And why have you become disturbed within me? (Psalm 42:3–5)

Unable to control his circumstances, he experienced feelings of despair and deep dismay.

Unresolved problems are like unresolved debts. You know they're there, but you just can't bring yourself to deal with them. You ignore the symptoms and suppress the reminders until they ulcerate the inner recesses of your soul. They deplete energy and cause a low-grade fever in your emotions. It won't be long before an overwhelming sense of helplessness and entrapment overshadows you.

Problems don't destroy you. *Unresolved* problems do. These are the nagging issues that create a breeding ground of fear. We feel compelled to live in the past and feel as if our hope for tomorrow is slipping away from us. Unresolved problems spawn chronic illness, work stress, relationship problems, and family breakdowns; any of these unwelcome life symptoms can trigger depression.

> "Character cannot be developed in ease and quiet. Only through experiences of trial and suffering can the soul be strengthened, vision cleared, ambition inspired, and success achieved."
>
> **HELEN KELLER**

Financial Stress

Financial problems will exacerbate depression. More than 50 percent of marital difficulties stem from financial disagreements. They trigger anger, arguments, a sense of hopelessness and exasperation, and lead to a bleak outlook on life. Financial problems also leach into decisions on the job and in the ministry, and cause you to overreact to expectations that are placed upon you.

Pressure to Excel

Moreover David was greatly distressed because the people spoke of stoning him, for all the people were embittered, each one because of his sons and his daughters. (1 Samuel 30:6)

Leaders are under a microscope. They become the culprit of choice and the scapegoat to blame. Recently I received a letter from a congregant saying that I wasn't doing my job since he was absent one Sunday and I didn't call on him to see if he was okay. He mentioned that in the last church he was attending, the pastor there didn't care either, and he suggested that this may have been the cause of his divorce! No matter what we do, some people are never satisfied. Feeling as if you're always letting people down can give you a huge dose of depression.

AN ACHE IN OUR SOUL

"Write your injuries in dust, your benefits in marble."

BENJAMIN FRANKLIN

One person described depression as an ache in our soul that finds its way into our body, our life, our marriage, and our ministry. Depression isn't simply an emotional problem. It leaches into every area of our life. While it may have prominent symptoms of sadness and melancholy behavior, it is far more than that. Depression is a real illness that needs to be treated, just as a bronchial infection needs prescription doses of an antibiotic.

> Restore to me the joy of Your salvation and sustain me with a willing spirit. (Psalm 51:12)

I do not claim to be a medical expert, so you will not find prescriptive advice on medications here. Medication may assist in the healing process to restore a sense of buoyancy, but it may not get you out of the water. If you don't deal with the underlying causes along with getting treatment, medication will be a temporary fix.

Research has concluded that neurotransmitters in the brain are reduced in clinically depressed individuals. Serotonin, one of these neurotransmitters, is a chemical courier that connects individual brain cells so that thoughts and emotions can occur normally.

Prescription antidepressants attempt to repair the chemical imbalance that causes depression. Certain medications aid in restoring balance and allow serotonin to gradually replenish itself. Many medications are available in today's pharmaceutical arsenal, but each program will need to begin with an accurate understanding of depression—and the type of medication that will best fit your situation.

Do you recognize any of these causes of depression in your own life? If so, you may be on the road to depression. You'll want to keep an eye out for the warning signs as we continue our walk together.

Come.

_____

Reflections

I am one of those pastors who have struggled with depression. I also have Hepatitis C. And I need to be honest and say that I still have bouts or struggles with depression today. I began taking a heavy daily dose of Interferon, and within four months, the hepatitis was no longer detectable. We celebrated, and I remained on treatment. In September 1999, I was informed that the hepatitis had returned. After thirteen months of treatment, I was devastated.

Our church began a stewardship campaign on September 9, 2001—two days before 9/11. Then during the building phase, a mistake in the estimating software and increasing building costs brought us in one million dollars over budget. We did a second stewardship campaign to bridge the gap. During this season, one of my closest friends died of lung cancer.

I began wondering where God was. I avoided people. I was able to do the critical tasks of ministry, but when it came to the important aspects of leadership, I balked. At those times, I wasn't even able to muster up the energy to make a phone call. I was so depressed at times that I couldn't even move. I would drive into the driveway and sit in my car with the engine running, unable to turn it off. I was so despondent that I wrestled with constant thoughts about dying. The family didn't get much of me. I'd go to bed early.

I was able to mask it pretty well. Not many knew. I still preached well and even included enough humor to have a good stage presence. But there was a growing disconnect between who I was up front and who I was in private.

One day I looked at my wife and said, "I have a problem and I need to do something about it." She already knew and had concerns. We talked through what I needed to do. Then I had to act on what we knew.

—PASTOR OF MIDWEST CHURCH

Chapter Four
Early Warning Signs

"The signs of approaching melancholy are . . . anguish and distress, dejection, silence, animosity . . . sometimes a desire to live and at other times a longing for death, suspicions on the part of the patient that a plot is being hatched against him."

CAELIUS AURELIANUS, METHODIST SCHOOL OF MEDICINE, AD FIFTH CENTURY

On December 26, 2004, a tsunami was generated by an earthquake off the shores of Indonesia measuring 9.1 on the Richter scale. The earthquake's epicenter was near Sumatra, Indonesia, and the resulting tsunami claimed more than 225,000 lives in eleven countries. It inundated some coastal towns with waves up to thirty meters (one hundred feet). Indonesia and Sri Lanka were among the hardest hit.

A few weeks later I joined a team from our church to do relief work in the area of Peraliya, on the southeast coast of Sri Lanka.

In partnership with other brave efforts, we set up temporary housing, built medical clinics, and distributed food. One dedicated Christian relief worker from Australia was Alison Thompson, Peraliya's "Angel of Mercy." She dressed in a batik skirt and a kurta-type top that reached to her worn-out slippers, and the villagers' fondness for her was obvious when we arrived. Together we worked hand-in-hand to bring hope and restore a future to these beleaguered people.

> "Acceptance of what has happened is the first step to overcoming the consequences of any misfortune."
>
> **WILLIAM JAMES**

Although we could do little to reverse what had already taken place, we could do something for the future. In an alliance with others, we paid for and set up an early warning system that would not only detect a possible tsunami but would also warn the people in time to evacuate the coastal regions for higher ground. Although tsunamis cannot be prevented, the early warning system will save lives and give them the edge.

WARNING SIGNS OF DEPRESSION

Early symptoms, if recognized, can signal the need to get help. A warning system doesn't necessarily prevent hitting the wall, but it will give you the edge and stamina to run through it. Paying attention to warning signs can help minimize the damage. The symptoms of depression can vary from person to person, but here are a few:

Sense of Hopelessness

Depressed people believe that life is not getting any better, and they see little hope for improvement. Their thoughts are tainted with pessimistic views of themselves, their futures look bleak, and their circumstances appear inescapable. They feel cursed by persistent sadness, apathy, and melancholy feelings of heaviness.

> "Hope begins in the dark, the stubborn hope that if you just show up and try to do the right thing, the dawn will come. You wait and watch and work: You don't give up."
>
> **ANNE LAMOTT**

Frequent Tears

Another early symptom is frequently feeling that events are out of control. A person can feel overwhelmed easily, bringing them to tears more often than usual.

Difficulty Concentrating

A very common symptom is the inability to stay focused for a prolonged period of time. Fatigue is never far away from a person wrestling with depression due to the emotional energy it takes to stay relational.

Decision Making Comes Hard

Depression counterbalances rational decision making with ambivalence and uncertainty. In these cases, the responsibility of decision making is often delegated to others.

Irritability

Symptoms of touchiness, a bad temper, and petulance accompany depression. These are simply further indications that a person is yearning for rest, renewal, and a season to heal. Not knowing if that is available, the depressed person will feel trapped and therefore angry at those around them.

Insomnia

Difficulty sleeping is one of the more common symptoms of depression. Although a desire to sleep in is common, getting to sleep can be difficult. It can contribute to the downward spiral that depression takes, leaving a person with less energy and a lowered interest in tomorrow's tasks. Once I got to sleep, however, getting up was equally as difficult. I wanted to stay in bed. Erratic sleep patterns may plague you as well.

Psalm 77 finds the psalmist, Asaph, in a similar state. He writes:

> "Anxiety does not empty tomorrow of its sorrows, but only empties today of its strength."
>
> **CHARLES H. SPURGEON**

When I remember God, then I am disturbed; when I sigh, then my spirit grows faint. . . . You have held my eyelids open; I am so troubled. (Psalm 77:3–4)

Asaph's confusion over events in his life caused him to blame God, and his incorrect conclusion resulted in a loss of hope . . . and a lot of tossing and turning in the wee hours of the morning.

Lowered Activity Levels

Depressed people have a decreased interest in group activities and a general lack of interest in life. Follow-through becomes increasingly difficult, and they find insufficient energy to solve problems or sustain ordinary levels of activity. God seems distant, and a previously relaxing activity (such as playing the guitar or piano) no longer brings the satisfaction it once did.

Feeling Alone

Caught in the vise of depressive feelings, Elijah felt like the loneliest man in the world.

I have been very zealous for the LORD, the God of hosts; for the sons of Israel have forsaken Your covenant, torn down Your altars and killed Your prophets with the sword. And I alone am left; and they seek my life, to take it away. (1 Kings 19:14)

Depressed, and desiring nothing more than a quick exit from life, Elijah somehow imagined that he was the last godly man on the planet. He felt as if he had no support—even though he had just been part of a fantastic miracle and gained the rousing support of God's people. He had allowed one evil woman to fill up his whole radar screen and ruin his outlook. But then God shared some information that must have stunned the melancholy prophet:

> "To overcome difficulties is to experience the full delight of existence."
>
> **ARTHUR SCHOPENHAUER**

Yet I will leave 7,000 in Israel, all the knees that have not bowed to Baal. (1 Kings 19:18)

God was saying, "I have 7,000 on your side, and you're letting one person sound like a million."

Oftentimes—especially when we're exhausted—we feel as if no one understands. We walk alone, our journey an arduous trudge through the valley of the shadow of death. The walls press in, skies remain leaden and dark, and loneliness dogs our every step.

Lack of Marital Attraction

Depression is often accompanied by a decrease in libido and a disinterest in your spouse—but not necessarily for sex itself. And that, my friend, is a dangerous combination.

With a growing desire for both isolation and release, a person becomes more vulnerable to pornography or affairs with someone they have no history with. The lesser the commitment, the higher the attraction. While the desire for immediate intimacy soars, the desire for prolonged commitment plunges. This can obviously create problems in marriage and family relationships.

The lesser the commitment, the higher the attraction.

Those suffering with depression often search for outlets in alcohol, affairs, drugs, or similar release points that give them a respite from the pain, temporary as it may be.

Eating Disorders

Some lose their appetites when they're depressed. Others can't stop eating. This problem can be mitigated if a person has a strict regimen or a spouse who keeps a regular schedule of meals. When depressed people are left to themselves, however, changes will be more evident.

Aches and Pains

Headaches, pains, and stomach ailments—including increased acid, ulcers, and heartburn—are common to the emotional state of anxiety and depression. In my case, hypertension and stress led to physical nerve damage in my neck. It was only with the help of a skilled therapist that I began to heal.

Other symptoms might visit you as well that are not mentioned here.

IT'S TIME TO LAUGH

You might enjoy these signs that signal you may be in the early stages of burnout or depression:

1. One year in solitary confinement is sounding more and more like a good option.
2. Spending time with your mother-in-law begins to be more inviting than going to work.
3. Your ministry leader calls for the third time wondering where you have been. You consider changing your phone number and possibly moving.
4. The sight of a ministry volunteer sign-up sheet brings on a severe allergic reaction.
5. You realize that you are in this ministry for life, which is funny, because you feel you no longer have one.

> "Through humor, you can soften some of the worst blows that life delivers. And once you find laughter, no matter how painful your situation might be, you can survive it."
>
> **BILL COSBY**

6. Every time somebody praises you for your work, you suspiciously eye them, certain that they will ask you to do one more thing.
7. You have contacted the Witness Protection Program to hide you from other ministry leaders.
8. You think you would like to work at McDonald's. It might be nice to see something more fried than you feel.
9. You imagine yourself in a monk's robe, and it doesn't seem so far-fetched anymore.
10. You find yourself seeing the long wait in line at the post office as a blessing from God.

GARDEN SEASONS

One final observation . . . We often wonder if Jesus knows what we are going through in our times of struggle and depression, but here in Luke, we can be assured that He does:

And being in agony He was praying very fervently; and His sweat became like drops of blood, falling down upon the ground. (Luke 22:44)

It was a season that compelled me into a winter wilderness that gave birth to a springtime of new growth that would refill my tank and renew my passion.

It might be a season where you find that your days are held in suspended animation and your soul is polarized. It was for me, but as I look back now, it was a season that compelled me into a winter wilderness that gave birth to a springtime of new growth that would refill my tank and renew my passion. But it took this season to bring me to a point where I too would say, "Father, if You are willing, remove this cup from Me; yet not My will, but Yours be done" (Luke 22:42).

———

Reflections

I had to deal with my burnout, but I didn't quite know how to process it with my staff. Our executive staff found my [situation] hard to deal with. But they bucked up and said, "Okay—take a break!" The rest of the staff knew to pray for me and that we were going through some things. It was hard for them to see me struggle. But the whole staff did a great job. It was the hardest couple of years of their lives.

The biggest issue they faced was the question of who was leading. They were leaderless and had to make decisions without me. Only once did they call for input. We all look back on it and say we are better off for the experience.

I left the day the staff told me to take time off. I was not emotionally able to process it with everyone just then. But when I returned, I gave a message on what a sabbatical is. They were all appreciative that I was back. So was I.

I still "flirt" with depression; I can feel it coming on. I look for the warning signs of what I call the slippery slope of depression.

When it comes near I have a choice. Sometimes you can feel like you don't have a choice and you can feel like a victim. But you do have a choice. Once you are in depression you can't get out of it easily. I believe it can become an addiction. Depression can become a comfort. You hate the low feeling, but there is something about despondency that is comforting. Depression can meet a need. You have to make a choice not to give in to it.

I read a book that helped me by Leanne Payne [The Healing Presence]. *She talked about the sin of introspection: when we stand beside ourselves and look at ourselves critically instead of looking at God and how He sees us. I have learned how to be gentle with myself, not to be critical, working on shame issues so that shame is not working itself into the gut level of who I am.*

—A Christian leader from California

Chapter Five
Solitary Refinement

"I wonder how much more effective our churches would be if we made the pastor's spiritual health—not the pastor's efficiency—our number one priority."

PHILIP YANCEY

The desert fathers went to the wilderness because the simplicity of life there offered few distractions. They quieted every demand and opened their ears to only One Voice. In the silent sands they turned to prayer and reconnection with God. Then when they were refreshed, they'd return to teach, counsel, make spiritual decisions, and provide pastoral care. In due time, they turned again to the desert for another period of refreshing. This oscillation between desert and ministry is a nonnegotiable pattern for today's busy pastor.

RETROSPECTION

Sequestered in the silence of my monastic cell, the dismantling process continued. The silent monks were busy about their duties, which left me free to ponder, reflect, and write. I filled dozens of legal pads with notes—confessions, cries of distress, and changes I knew I'd have to make in my life. Some things would have to change *right away*, other refinements would be completed *within the year*, and still other long-term modifications would extend *into the coming decade*. At the top of my list were personal health issues. I needed to recognize the trigger points in my personality that brought me to where I was: An inability to say no. Overachieving, and then the guilty feeling that I was not attaining what I felt was expected of me.

> "Quietude, which some men cannot abide because it reveals their inward poverty, is as a palace of cedar to the wise, for along its hallowed courts the King in His beauty deigns to walk."
>
> **CHARLES H. SPURGEON**

I knew I needed to restructure the way I lived. It would not be an immediate change. It would eventuate. But I needed to find a way to navigate the colliding feelings that would accost me along the way and attempt to bushwhack me back to old default settings. I had to plot my course and stick with it.

Some days I would write out my thoughts for hours, page after yellow page, detailing my pain and my discouragement. At other times, when my inner ache and tenderness refused rational explanation, I would simply stare for hours into the surrounding coastal forest.

Solitude is a chosen separation for refining your soul. Isolation is what you crave when you neglect the first.

When I returned from my little self-imposed exile, I knew I would somehow have to rearrange a host of drivers in my thinking and activities, learning what filled and what drained my tank. I had to learn how to recognize the symptoms and be more preventive than medicinal. It would require either a new line of work or a new way of thinking.

I would opt for a new way of thinking.

The days I spent at the monastery taught me the difference between solitude and isolation. They may contain similar characteristics, but in reality they are worlds apart. Solitude is a chosen separation for refining your soul. Isolation is what you crave when you neglect the first.

For several days I pondered and recorded what God was revealing to me. Were there trigger points I wasn't aware of? Were there warning signs I was clearly aware of but ignored? I had to evaluate what brought me to the cliff's edge . . . and what took me over.

Sometimes we get so busy rowing the boat, we don't take the time to stop and see where we're going . . . or what we are becoming.

It's a little difficult to describe those days. It was like looking in the mirror and being introduced to myself for the first time in a few years—and to what I had become. Sometimes we get so busy rowing the boat, we don't take the time to stop and see where we're going . . . or what we are becoming. I needed some transforming. I wanted to be able to get up in the morning, look in the mirror, and *like* the person I was becoming.

But at that time, I didn't.

If you return, then I will restore you—before Me you will stand; and if you extract the precious from the worthless, you will become My spokesman. (Jeremiah 15:19)

Alone in the monastery, I began a retrospective journey. God surfaced personal fears and false assumptions that I had retained as truth for many years. These weren't necessarily sins in my life, but their overall effects seemed every bit as destructive.

In the ministry of shepherding people, we learn to depend on such tools as insight, intuition, judgment, and discernment. Developing and honing these skills makes for a great leader, but if unguarded, it opens the door to under-processed conclusions and inaccurate assumptions. The ability to precisely define reality is the starting point for any hope for equilibrium.

In the first two days at the monastery, I searched for triggers that could have begun the downward journey that caused the shrinkage of my soul. I had to find those culprits, those hidden snares that had tripped me up again and again. The evenings went long, and the days crawled by. The answers I desperately needed eluded me. I think God did this so that I would journey farther down the road with Him, perhaps discovering so much more than I had set out to look for in the first place.

> "Prosperity is a great teacher; adversity a greater."
>
> **WILLIAM HAZLITT**

MILES WITHOUT MAINTENANCE

In 2006, the Federal Aviation Administration grounded all DC-10s because on one flight the engine fell off, resulting in the death of 213 passengers. This unthinkable flaw didn't take place overnight; it was the result of successive times of ignored maintenance.

When my wheels fell off, I knew that it was due to a long-standing practice of disregarding certain feelings of inadequacy, discouragement, and anger. I could no longer afford to ignore these things or tolerate them as unresolved issues in my life. The investigation began, and with the insight and direction of

SOLITARY REFINEMENT - **73**

God's Spirit, I found vulnerabilities that I had overlooked for too many years.

My father was a first sergeant in the army, and he disciplined us kids in the patriotic way. He laid down the stripes and we saw stars! I felt the need to perform, to succeed, to endure and win at any cost. That was one embedded principle I needed to unlearn. I had not taken the time to reassess my motivations and the unseen drivers that propelled me forward. The monastery was my opportunity to do that.

I kept searching and searching for common denominators in my life that had been rubbing raw patches on my soul.

I also had to determine—to really settle in my soul—what I would actually be held accountable for in my life.

But there was something else.

I also had to determine—to really settle in my soul—what I would actually be held accountable for in my life. The Scriptures say, "You will always have the poor among you" (Matthew 26:11 NLT), so I knew that there were some issues that may never be resolved, no matter how hard I tried.

CONCERNS OR RESPONSIBILITIES?

For whatever reason, some of us tend to worry. If there isn't enough to worry about in our own family, we look to our neighbor's family. If we don't find something to worry us with our neighbor's family, we'll send out our worry net even wider, to a family in a neighboring state . . . or another country. If we knew people on the southern hemisphere of Mars, we'd probably worry about them too.

When a concern about another's performance or a lack of leadership at work arises, we begin tracking it as if it were a *personal responsibility*. As a result, we worry about it, gossip in the lunchroom, and make it the topic of our conversation.

It may be a legitimate *concern*, but it is not our responsibility.

Don't rush past that last sentence. *Learning the difference between a concern and a responsibility may save your ministry, your family, and your sanity.*

If we mis-define concerns as personal responsibilities, it will eventually confuse us and diffuse our energies.

> Like one who takes a dog by the ears is he who passes by and meddles with strife not belonging to him. (Proverbs 26:17)

Concerns could be things like:

- A neighbor's messy yard

- A teacher's inability to keep the students' attention

- What we think others feel about us

> "The happiest people I know are the ones who have learned how to hold everything loosely and have given the worrisome, stress-filled, fearful details of their lives into God's keeping."
>
> **CHARLES R. SWINDOLL**

So what in the world do we do with something that concerns us? We intercede. We supplicate. We bring it before God in prayer and lay it at His feet—and we may do this a couple dozen times a day. Then the Lord says, "I'll take it from here." Read this passage from Philippians as though you were encountering it for the first time.

Always be full of joy in the Lord. I say it again—rejoice! Let everyone see that you are considerate in all you do. Remember, the Lord is coming soon.

Don't worry about anything; instead, pray about everything. Tell God what you need, and thank him for all he has done. Then you will experience God's peace, which exceeds anything we can understand. His peace will guard your hearts and minds as you live in Christ Jesus. (Philippians 4:4–7 NLT)

You could go to a million therapists and spend the fortune of Bill Gates and not get better advice than that. *Don't worry about anything . . . pray about everything.* So many of my worries have come from my inability (or unwillingness) to discern between a *concern* and a *responsibility*. I had mixed them up, and as a result, the world was resting on my shoulders.

If you had only one month left to live, you'd be surprised at all the things that really didn't matter anymore.

The Bible directs us to take our concerns to the feet of Jesus and leave them there, while we invest our time and emotional energy in the things that truly are our responsibilities.

That was the target I needed to start hitting in my life. But I was still a long way from the bull's-eye.

WHAT MATTERS MOST

A funny thing happened while I was spilling my thoughts onto paper. Those yellow pads became my confidants, my shrinks, my counselors, the ones who would listen long enough for me to confront my own fears and answer my own questions.

I remember something from my high school math class. In order to solve certain equations, you had to find the common denominator, and that would be the starting point for arriving at the answer. I knew I had to do that in my life as well.

Imagine it this way: If you had only one month left to live, you'd be surprised at all the things that really didn't matter anymore:

What a co-worker said to you in anger
That loan your friend has failed to repay
The time your boss overlooked you for a raise
The fact that someone else got the office with the window

If you had thirty days to live, these sorts of issues would have no importance to you. Bringing them up would seem absurd, almost obscene. Savoring life, squeezing the very most out of each and every precious day, would be far more important to you.

Is life any less precious because we don't know how much of it we have left?

I knew that to get the answers I was seeking, I would have to distill my life down to the few issues of absolute importance—items that would influence me and direct my energies and efforts for the rest of my life. I had to come to grips with what *only I could accomplish.* These things could not be delegated, ignored, or sloughed off onto someone else. These would be responsibilities that, in the end, God would hold me accountable for.

I had to come to grips with what *only I could accomplish.*

Brian Dyson, the former COO of Coca-Cola, delivered the commencement address at Georgia Tech in 1996. In it he gave a simile that explained the distinctions of what is most important in life:

Imagine life as a game in which you are juggling some five balls in the air. You name them—work, family, health, friends, and spirit—and you are keeping all of these in the air. You will soon understand that work is a rubber ball. If you drop it, it will bounce back. But the other four balls—family, health, friends, and spirit—are made of glass. If you drop one of these, they will be irrevocably scuffed, marked, nicked, damaged, or even shattered. They will never be the same. You must understand that and strive for balance in your life.

It was only by God's grace that He gave me another chance to redeem my drops and faltering. Even so, I had a job to do. It was time—really, past time—to identify the most important priorities of my life.

It was time—really, past time—to identify the most important priorities of my life.

THE MOST IMPORTANT FIVE PERCENT

If you and I are going to enjoy healing and rest at our very core, *we must discover and discern the top 5 percent of life.* I allude to this crucial principle in my book *The Divine Mentor,* but let me briefly summarize it here.

Eighty-five percent of what we do, anyone can do: checking e-mail, answering messages, attending meetings, reading the newspaper or trade journals, and making simple decisions. These tasks don't require an elite expertise or specialized skill. Many of these tasks can be delegated to others so we can concentrate on what's most important to the job we have been given to do.

Ten percent of what we do, someone with a modicum of training should be able to accomplish. After all, if we were trained to do what we do, someone else of like capability could learn how to run the computer program, solve the problem, lead the meeting, or do the tasks that we do. With appropriate schooling and experience, someone else can perform a surgery, manage an engineering project, or sell real estate. Certain aspects of these activities can be assigned to trained individuals.

But 5 percent of what I do, only *I* can do! *This the most important 5 percent for me.* I can't delegate these initiatives to anyone else. I can't hire someone else to take my place in any of these activities because they require that *I* be there! This 5 percent will determine the validity of the other 95 percent. This is what I had to discover and make as the epicenter of my life.

> "As sure as God puts His children in the furnace He will be in the furnace with them."
>
> **CHARLES H. SPURGEON**

My 5 percent may differ from yours, but the principle is trans-ferrable to everyone—married, single, widowed, old, or young. It is true for those with children, empty nesters, or young couples just starting out in life.

I had to rethink what was most important to me—what God had asked *me* to do—and how I would restructure my life to concentrate on these priorities in my final stretch. I had to think what my last 5 percent would include. What were the things that only I could do and, if neglected, would affect the rest of my life? Here are the responsibilities I wrote down:

1. A vibrant, growing relationship with my Lord and Savior, Jesus Christ
2. A healthy and genuine relationship with my spouse
3. An authentic family that is close to God and close to one another
4. A God-pleasing ministry
5. A physically healthy body and a creative soul
6. Taking time to enjoy life with family and friends

These six items require a daily investment of my time and heart. In fact, the condition of these six areas will, to a large extent, determine the state of my life. If these areas are compromised, the consequences will be felt in other areas. If this 5 percent fell into disrepair or neglect, my life would grind to a halt until these priorities were once again restored.

WHAT SHAPES OUR SOULS

We often fill our days with the 85 percent because it requires so little of us. We then dip into the next 10 percent. But during this season of burnout, even that drained me completely. I had nothing left for the crucial 5 percent, knowing that this would require the most of me.

We won't be held accountable for how much we have done, but for how much we have done of what *He has asked us to do*.

And the crucial 5 percent is what God will one day hold you accountable for. It will not necessarily be the 85 percent that will shape your future, or the 10 percent that will build your legacy. It may impress the world, it may burnish your résumé, but it won't impress God as much as that all-important 5 percent. Your choice of what is most important will shape your soul.

We won't be held accountable for how much we have done, but for how much we have done of what *He has asked us to do*.

What makes up your most important 5 percent? Identify them and write them down.

1.

2.

3.

4.

5.

6.

MAKING CHOICES EASY

With everything else demanding your attention and time, the 5 percent can get tangled up in a battle of choices. But there can be no competition for this.

You will have to make many choices in order to balance your life—choices with regard to your time, management style, invitations you accept, how you spend your leisure, and how to prioritize.

I wish these choices could be easy. It would be wonderful if God would remove the doubts and risks and replace them with confidence and guarantees. But it doesn't work that way.

I remember a story told of a small airline. On a four-hour flight, the flight attendant approached one of the passengers and asked him if he would like to have dinner.

"What are my choices?" he asked.

The flight attendant replied: *"Yes or no."*

Choice becomes more difficult when you have to make a decision between two options of equal value.

Choice becomes more difficult when you have to make a decision between two options of equal value: Shall I wear the red or the blue outfit, dress casually or formally, have dinner at home or dine out, strawberry or vanilla, one job or another?

On the other hand, if you can raise one option so that it towers far above the other, the decision becomes considerably easier.

What if the choice were between life and death, staying in a burning house or getting out, making $10 an hour or $500 an hour to do the same job?

The greater the difference, the easier the choice.

So how far above the rest is your all-important 5 percent?

Just above the 95 percent is not enough. Give it the highest importance you can, and the choices become very easy. If you allow it to compete with the other 95 percent, the choices become very hard. That's when you begin to compromise and make mistakes that put you into spiritual and relational debt.

> "Sometimes, struggles are exactly what we need in our life. If we were to go through life without any obstacles, we would be crippled. We would not be as strong as what we could have been. Give every opportunity a chance, leave no room for regrets."
>
> **AUTHOR UNKNOWN**

Nothing becomes a life change until you assign the highest value you can to it. Your faith, your marriage, your family, and your health have to be not only priorities, but higher priorities than everything else, including work, money, promotion, or position.

ANCHORS OF MY LIFE

Thomas à Kempis wrote: "A good, devout person first arranges inwardly the things to be done outwardly. . . . Who has a fiercer struggle than the person who strives to master himself? And this must be our occupation: to strive to master ourselves and daily to grow stronger and advance for good."

In the spirit of the good monk's words, one of the best things I have done in my life is to establish values *before* I have had to make major decisions. There must be certain pilings driven so deeply into my soul that in times of crisis they will serve as immovable, unquestionable anchors of my life. Without these, everything is up for grabs and every value challenged.

> **There must be certain pilings driven so deeply into my soul that in times of crisis they will serve as immovable, unquestionable anchors in my life.**

Here are some questions I asked myself in order to establish parameters *before* I found myself in the situation:

- Is there ever a time when sex outside of marriage can be an option?
- Is there ever a reason to abandon my family?
- Can I indulge in immorality and still keep my faith intact?

Are these things negotiable? Under any circumstances?

If I haven't firmly made up my mind and established my convictions *before* I come up against any such situations in my life, they may very well become "options." I might toy with the ideas in my mind . . . or I might even give in. But if I have already determined certain boundaries, driving them deep into the soil of my soul, then these sorts of questions will hit and bounce away—like tennis balls against a brick wall.

In the press of the moment, you and I need to have certain questions answered in our souls before they are ever asked. Balance begins at the very core of our being. Settling the interior part of me is crucial to living a balanced life. Why? Because it's the hardest part of me to control!

OKAY, I GOT IT . . .

The days I spent in the monastery passed—very slowly—and my soul began to catch up with my body. The pain subsided a bit, enough for me to function normally. I even found myself laughing at the monks in their hooded robes, whispering when the bishop wasn't around. I found humor in the old story of a novitiate monk who was allowed only two words a year. After the first year, he stood before the bishop and chose his two words carefully: "Bed hard!"

> "I thank God for my handicaps, for through them, I have found myself, my work, and my God."
>
> **HELEN KELLER**

At the end of the second year, his summary of the year was: "Food bad."

The third year found him again standing before the bishop, and his final comment was: "I quit!"

"Good!" the bishop shot back. "All you've done since coming here is complain, complain, complain!"

GOING STIR-CRAZY

By about the fifth day with the monks, I started feeling my oats again. I was tiring of no coffee, no Internet, no phones, and no talking. I needed a break from the silence. I live in Honolulu near Waikiki, the Hawaiian city that never sleeps. I needed some coffee and conversation! My program called for two more days of silence, and the hooded monks didn't look like they would be open to substitutions in the menu.

The following day I attended the morning prayers at five. After the early mass of communion and Gregorian chant, the devotees would embark on solemn ceremony back in their rooms. Assured that each was safely behind closed doors, I decided to make my escape . . . at least for one day. I needed civilization. I needed caffeine!

I drove slowly out of the compound, feeling like a guilty dog that had just dug under the backyard fence. I made it to the highway and headed north to the last town inhabited by humans. Over an hour later, my cell phone revived and welcomed me with a beep that I had voicemail waiting. Within minutes, I came to the beautiful town of Carmel—and to an even more beautiful Internet café. The heavens had opened! I drank six cups of coffee, answered all my waiting e-mails, and sent notes to loved ones, notifying them of my survival. I even wrote to people I didn't know.

Still hungry for interaction, I called my assistant in Hawaii and in hushed tones said: "Hello! This is Wayne."

My assistant said, "Why are you whispering?"

"Shhhhh!" I hushed him. Looking around with a guilty scan, I said with a muffled voice, "I escaped!"

I felt like a schoolboy playing hooky. "I couldn't stand it," I told him. "They're nice, but I just had to take a break. They don't ever talk! It's driving me crazy!"

"Was it hard sneaking out?" he asked.

"No," I quipped, "but getting back in will be!"

By dusk I knew I had to head back. I could imagine angry monks with their hooded scowls, their eyes glowing, waiting for the return of the stray.

When I later shared this escapade with my wife, she asked, "When they found out that you left for the day, were they angry with you?"

"I don't know," I replied with a wry smile. "Till this day, they've never said anything."

> "God 'resources' us even when ministry depletes us. God enables us when ministry baffles us. God makes us sufficient for every situation we encounter for Him."
>
> *PASTORS AT GREATER RISK*

IF I COULD DO IT ALL OVER AGAIN

Since my experience at the monastery, I have asked myself: "If I could live my life all over again, what would I do differently?"

My, what things we would do differently! We could avoid the mistakes that cost us years of grief, and we could sidestep the potholes that jarred our teeth and caught us unawares. We would make wiser decisions in our marriages and care more deeply for those we love.

Obviously, this whole "leading on empty" juncture in my life was accompanied by deep emotional pain and a wrenching sense of disorientation. But Romans 8:28 hadn't disappeared from the Bible, and in my heart of hearts, I knew the Lord who loved me could work through even these circumstances for my good.

In fact, I could already begin to see a few fragile sprouts of new growth pressing through the parched soil. This strange period of my life held out some promise in the midst of the pain; I just had to start looking at it differently. I was looking at the next twenty-five-year stretch of my life, and I knew I had been given another chance to change things. I had the fresh opportunity to choose to rewrite my future or default back to the same-old, same-old.

> "Continuous effort—not strength or intelligence—is the key to unlocking our potential."
>
> **WINSTON CHURCHILL**

I decided to make a choice; I would do it better this time.

———

Reflections

Working through my burnout was a two-year journey. It was like a grieving process. My first wife was killed in a car accident. I learned that in the midst of grief, the deep pain gets spaced farther and farther apart as healing gradually occurs. It was that way with depression for me. The frequency of depression moves farther apart. Today I find that when I am approaching a depressed place, I have tools to get myself out.

The goal is not to "get over depression" quickly. The goal is to draw close to God. When my focus is on God, I am helped tremendously. Then I can find the positive things to look at that lift my spirit.

Depression is often a birthing process just before God makes a breakthrough. If you can look at depression as a gift and look at what God is going to do in you through it in the future, it can change your perspective about it.

I have had to work on rhythms of life so I don't get depleted. I make sure I am getting enough sleep at night. I try to eat the right kinds of foods. I have learned that I need replenishing friends who are safe. I make sure that I have those kinds of friends.

At the church, we've established what we call "working time away" or study breaks. I can relieve the pressure by not working in the office when I need to work on some creative things. Last year we started "extended time away" or mini-sabbaticals. Last year I took the entire summer off to spend time with my family.

—PASTOR ON THE EAST COAST

Chapter Six
Finding the Still Waters

"He maketh me to lie down in green pastures: he leadeth me beside the still waters. He restoreth my soul."

PSALM 23:2–3 KJV

"And just what would I *do* on this 'break' you suggest?"

I had returned from my monastery experience, but I was far from being out of the forest. There was much work yet to be done. *Knowing the remedy* doesn't necessarily complete the healing; the difference comes when we *apply* it. *Reading the menu* doesn't fill you up; *eating the food* does.

Knowing the remedy doesn't necessarily complete the healing; the difference comes when we *apply* it.

> "Wisdom is the right use of knowledge. To know is not to be wise. Many men know a great deal, and are all the greater fools for it. There is no fool so great a fool as a knowing fool. But to know how to use knowledge is to have wisdom."
>
> **CHARLES H. SPURGEON**

I knew the menu, but now it was time to dig in.

I had returned from my time at the monastery with a list of important changes to make in my life, but I hadn't really started yet. I could see my destination somewhere out there on the horizon, but I hadn't begun the journey. I knew the answers, but I still couldn't connect the dots.

NO MORE LEADING ON EMPTY

"Your soul," my psychologist friend explained, "is like a battery that discharges each time you give life away, and it needs to be recharged regularly. You haven't given it time to recharge, and that doesn't happen overnight. It's a gradual, slow recharge."

> **Your soul is like a battery that discharges each time you give life away, and it needs to be recharged regularly.**

He pressed me to take a year off, but that seemed impossible. Even six months seemed excessive. I had agreed to take two months off in the summer. It was longer than I had ever taken and seemed strange (at first). But soon it would become an annual ritual that would actually serve to increase my shelf life, enlarge my ministry's fruitfulness, and help raise up emerging leaders waiting on the sidelines.

"So how do I recharge my soul?" I asked.

"For two months, do as many of the things that fill your tank as you can. That is how you recharge."

Each of us has an internal emotional reservoir. On the topside, there's an input, and on the bottom, a drain. Certain activities will drain you more than fill you, and others will fill you more than drain you. Some tasks will contribute to you and others will take from you.

When I speak and teach, it fills my tank. When I counsel, it drains my tank. For others, it may be just the opposite. When I play certain sports, I am renewed. When I have to organize them, I am depleted.

Do as many of the things that fill your tank as you can. That is how you recharge.

What fills you? What drains you? Or thinking back to a decades-old Exxon ad, what puts a tiger in your tank?

You need to know the difference.

I couldn't procrastinate any longer. I needed to grab myself by the shirt collar, sit myself down with pen and paper, and determine exactly (without guilt) which activities filled and replenished my emotional tank, and which ones pulled the plug and drained me dry.

Here is a short list I made of those things that tend to refresh me and fill me:

"Be aware of wonder. Live a balanced life—learn some and think some and draw and paint and sing and dance and play and work every day some."

ROBERT FULGHUM

- sports
- traveling
- reading
- devotional time
- golfing
- dinners with my wife, Anna

- music
- creatively utilizing the arts for the gospel
- some speaking
- training leaders

Equally important, I also duly recorded those activities that drain and deplete me, including . . .

- excessive counseling
- unresolved home problems
- unnecessary paper work
- working with people who disdain change
- managing instead of leading
- constant deadlines placed on me by others
- working with staff that leave unfinished assignments

The busier I became, the less time I had for activities that replenished me.

Here are the hard facts: The busier I became, the less time I had for activities that replenished me. I couldn't play sports because there were deadlines I had to meet. I couldn't find time to read because I had sermons to prepare. I couldn't get out on the golf course because other "more critical" demands made golfing seem like "time wasting" leisure. When I did brush the cobwebs off my clubs and carve out a round of golf, I noticed what should have been obvious: My scores accurately reflected my intermittent play. Imagine that! And it's a problem that still lingers to this day!

You can get along for a while with "more drain than fill," but it will eventually catch up with you. It's like a car that someone drives for years without an oil change. You might squeeze twenty or thirty thousand miles out of it, but the neglect will come at the price of an engine that grinds to a stop.

That's the course I was on, and even though the red lights kept flashing on my instrument panel, I couldn't stop. Or wouldn't.

I was leading on empty. And I couldn't keep it up much longer.

Write down what fills your tank and what drains it. List at least six things in each category.

Fills   Drains

_____   _____

_____   _____

_____   _____

_____   _____

_____   _____

_____   _____

Have your spouse do the same, then share your lists over a nice evening dinner. Exchange the lists: You take your spouse's and he/she takes yours. Then for the next three months, use that list as your prayer list, promising to help each other by encouraging what fills your tanks and doing what you can to alleviate what drains the other's tank.

> "God will one day hold us each accountable for all the things He created for us to enjoy, but we refused to do so."
>
> **RABBINIC SAYING**

LIFE IN TANDEM

All of this process of breakdown and recovery—self-absorbing as it tended to be—wasn't just about me. I also needed to know what filled my wife's tank and what drained her dry. Pursuing this knowledge saved my sanity—and may have saved our marriage as well.

When we first moved to Hawaii, we bid adieu to our family and friends in Oregon, where my wife's parents lived. We had two children by then and really felt terrible about separating the little ones from their adoring grandparents. So in a valiant effort to keep her family connected, Anna would call her mother every few days to converse about the children's school activities, the weather, and anything else that came to mind.

After a few months of these frequent long-distance chats, I noticed that Ma Bell was taking a larger and larger portion of my paycheck. (With the salary of a novice pastor, there wasn't much to begin with.) On one occasion, after opening the dreaded monthly invoice, I stormed into the kitchen and announced to my startled wife: "You're taking me to the poorhouse! This bill is over a hundred and fifty dollars! No more! From now on, if you want to talk to your mother, have her call you. Otherwise, call her collect!" Out of compassion, I added, "Feel free to do that once a week."

> "The family is one of nature's masterpieces."
>
> **GEORGE SANTAYANA**

My wife humbly complied. But after a couple of months, I noticed a change in her normally demure disposition. She was becoming the wicked witch of the north. Our relationship was soon strained and our conversations became icy.

I failed to recognize that one of the activities that filled her tank the most had been those frequent conversations with her mother. As the only daughter in her family, she was a happy lady when their relationship was close and vibrant. But by cutting that off, I became an adversary rather than an advocate.

When I finally understood the imbalance, we made some necessary and immediate changes. I realized that 150 dollars each month is a small price to pay for a happy wife, and Anna soon returned to the beautiful lady I had married. About a year and a half later, both her father and mother passed away, and I dread to think where my marriage would be today if I had missed this lesson.

Learn what fills and drains your tank as well as that of your spouse, and it could save you years of sleeping in the doghouse—not to mention strain on your ministry.

> "Year by year the complexities of this spinning world grow more bewildering, and so each year we need all the more to seek peace and comfort in the joyful simplicities."
>
> *WOMAN'S HOME COMPANION*, **DECEMBER 1935**

WARNING LIGHTS

At this juncture, let me add a slight clarification. We all realize that there will be tensions in any occupation—whether it is banking, child care, or nuclear engineering. There will inevitably be those stress points you can't wish away. While tensions eventually have to be faced and addressed appropriately, there are some stressors you may have to live with for a long time before you figure out how to resolve them.

We're all involved in a smorgasbord of daily activities—some we choose, others are chosen for us. In your job, in ministry, and in your family, there will inevitably be those activities that tend to deplete you. It's impossible to completely avoid things that drain you. But by making sure you keep your emotional tank topped off, you won't find yourself suddenly facing a flashing "low fuel" light on your inner instrument panel.

Difficulty With Decision Making

What does that low-fuel warning look like? In my case, I found myself struggling over decisions that used to come easily. I wanted nothing to do with problem solving of any kind, and if

I suspected that a particular issue would demand something of me, I would procrastinate in dealing with it.

Increasing Allures

I recognized something else: Temptations and distractions seemed more alluring than before. In the press of life, if there aren't sufficient and appropriate escapes, we become susceptible to unsuitable ones.

In Luke 4, Jesus gives us a lesson in life essentials. Concerning His marathon forty-day fast, the biblical account says: "He ate nothing during those days, and when they had ended, *He became hungry. And the devil said to Him . . .*" (Luke 4:2–3).

It's no accident that the Evil One came calling in our Savior's moment of human vulnerability. That's his usual plan of attack. That's Temptation 101. The adversary lurks in the shadows of vulnerable moments in our lives. Like an uncomplaining sniper squatting in a darkened second-story room, he squints patiently into his high-powered scope, waiting for an opportune time to squeeze off a shot at his unsuspecting target.

We all need emotional steam valves to let off pressure. When the stresses of life press in, if we can't equalize the pressure, the external weight overwhelms us. Without appropriate ways to fill our tanks, we become prone to unhealthy substitutes. Affairs, casual pornography, excessive alcohol, prescription medication, or illicit drugs—all are counterfeit stand-ins that lure us into unhealthy, tragic choices.

If we ignore or mask the building anxiety we feel, our emotional tanks drain even further. The next stage brings more intensified symptoms. This is where I found myself on the curbside crying. With my emotions thinned to a razor's edge, my hypersensitivity heightened my desire to retreat. I avoided the office and withdrew from anyone who required anything of me.

Desire for Isolation

As I've already mentioned, desire for isolation in these times differs from a deliberate period of solitude and reflection. Solitude is a healthy and prescriptive discipline; isolation is a symptom of emotional depletion. As a pastor, I noticed the temptations to escape increasing by the day, and I desperately looked for replenishment outside of the church . . . or from *within* the church.

Solitude is a healthy and prescriptive discipline; isolation is a symptom of emotional depletion.

With the presence of these symptoms, we know that our filling lags far behind our draining, and corrective measures must be taken immediately. If not, we will slip into the worst of scenarios—the state of mind we sometimes refer to as "nervous breakdown."

This final stage of emptiness can cut the legs out from under a leader's ministry and future potential. Navigating back to normalcy from this point becomes nothing short of a miracle. Finally giving way under an extended onslaught of stress and anxiety and a serious imbalance of chemistry, a man or woman's mental condition undergoes meltdown. This demands medical attention and treatment.

A WORD TO SHEPHERDS

By the way, shepherd-leaders are a unique group. They don't fit in the tidy boxes occupied by hundreds of other business categories. I realize that there may be many similarities between corporate principles and church work, but when it comes to the rare and inimitable calling of a shepherd, some critical distinctions need to be addressed.

There will always be a tension between what I do and who I am because they run so closely together. A minister isn't like a salesman who stops talking business after five o'clock or a dockworker who refuses to pick up a fallen box because he's off the clock. He doesn't live in the world of a retiring politician, who contents himself with leaving unfinished items for his successor.

There will always be a tension between what I do and who I am because they run so closely together.

A shepherd-leader is more like a country doctor. Regardless of the time of day, when people are experiencing symptoms of appendicitis or when a baby needs birthing, he can't say, "I'm off duty. I punched out at five." In a sense, a pastor never punches out. Of course some may, but for those who see their profession as a *calling,* they simply cannot.

> "I find that doing the will of God leaves me no time for disputing about His plans."
>
> **GEORGE MACDONALD**

What I do *is* who I am, and who I am is inextricably connected to what I do. I am a shepherd. It wasn't something I chose as a business profession. It was something I could not escape!

John 15:16 reminds me: "You did not choose Me but I chose you, and appointed you that you would go and bear fruit, and that your fruit would remain."

Pastoring people is not a business. It's a life calling. It's who you are, and who you are (in this case) is inescapably tied to what you do.

It will be incumbent upon each of us to *navigate* that tension rather than try to remove it. There will be dichotomies in every life calling, and this will be one that each minister must confront and resolve before he or she traverses too far down the pathway that shepherds travel.

HE LEADETH ME . . .

I began to find still waters and places where I could lie down in green pastures. But these places of repose were dependent upon principles of cadence and sustainability: *cadence* because my life would now require an intentional and measured rhythm to replace the knee-jerk urgencies that had dictated my schedule, and *sustainability* because I could not do this for a few months and then revert back to the way I used to live. This required intentionality and insight gained from past experiences.

> "I gave my life to this little group of people. No one *took* it. I gave it willingly, and I'd gladly give them another lifetime if I had it to give."
>
> **A VETERAN PASTOR IN** *PASTORS AT GREATER RISK*

TAKING TIME FOR REFLECTION

Our lives are like notebooks. Some are lived with empty pages—nothing is written down. Others are filled with experiences, but once they are recorded, they are never visited again. The best lives are like notebooks whose writings are read and reflected upon over and over again. Lessons are extracted and futures are reassessed.

What I do *is* who I am, and who I am is inextricably connected to what I do.
I am a shepherd.

Experience alone will not make us wiser. When we repeat a mistake, experience only reminds us that we made this same blunder before. But experience *plus reflection* will grant us insight, and insight helps us to grow and change.

Pain is inevitable. Misery is not. You see, pain is a result of loving deeply and living fully. Misery, on the other hand, is a result of living without reflecting and trying to forge our future without insight.

> "Fiery trials make golden Christians."
>
> **CHARLES H. SPURGEON**

I received advice from my psychologist friend but still delayed making any life-changing decisions. Many times we won't make major course corrections until the pain of staying the same becomes greater than the pain of making the change.

And I began to feel the pain in my chest.

Reflections

Dear Dr. Cordeiro,

When I attended your Hawaii Leadership Practicum two years ago, I was eight months into the darkest and most painful season of my life and ministry. I had been deeply wounded in ministry and was trying to heal while doing my best to appear strong for the congregation. Momentum was dropping and I was simply hanging on, hoping this darkness would lift. I was meeting with a Christian psychologist but still felt deeply depressed. I lacked vision and energy and I felt far from God. I had slipped into maintaining and managing the church. I had nothing left to give. I had no compassion for people.

It was not until some months later that I was referred to a different Christian psychologist in my area, who specializes in depression and anxiety. I was diagnosed with clinical depression. As I reflected on my past I realized that I had suffered from clinical depression for most of my life (including my childhood) and never knew it. I just thought how I felt was normal. Because I was strong and could persevere through challenges, I kept pushing through the snowstorm, determined to find victory.

I immediately began treatment, which included counseling, medication, and reading lots of books on the subject. By God's grace, a good counselor, and the support of a few trusted friends, I am beginning to enjoy ministry again. I have experienced a new dimension of God's grace, peace, and joy. I have a new passion for ministry, greater energy, a greater sense of purpose and fulfillment, and a greater love for people.

—PASTOR FROM CALIFORNIA

Chapter Seven
The New Perspective

"The eye is the lamp of the body; so then if your eye is clear, your whole body will be full of light. But if your eye is bad, your whole body will be full of darkness. If then the light that is in you is darkness, how great is the darkness!"

Matthew 6:22–23

I was sure it was my heart.

My erratic pulse continued until I felt compelled to call a doctor and check myself in for a thorough heart exam.

The doctor began with an electrocardiogram, then a stress test. With wires attached to my chest, I began a slow pace on a treadmill turning a three-foot-wide belt under my feet. In steady increments, the belt revolved faster and faster and the incline increased, simulating a steep uphill walk. The doctor watched both my pace as well as a graph taking shape on a strip of paper.

As my heart responded to differing levels of stress, the doctor made several notations on his clipboard. Beads of sweat began to form on my brow, but he assured me that my heart seemed strong and vital.

Then he cranked the thing up even more!

It was only under these conditions of physical stress that my physician could determine the true strength of my heart and whether it was sturdy enough to cope with life's pressures. Although my physical heart checked out fine, I learned a life lesson that I would not soon forget. It might seem like a paradox, but for the heart to grow stronger, it must undergo stress.

CONVERTING BAD INTO GOOD

> "I've missed more than 9,000 shots in my career. I've lost almost 300 games. Twenty-six times, I've been trusted to take the game-winning shot and missed. I've failed over and over and over again in my life. And that is why I succeed."
>
> **MICHAEL JORDAN**

As much as I wanted to avoid the pain of depression and its accompanying de-motivation, God would use those very things to build within me an even stronger heart and lifestyle. Something wondrous happens when we draw aside and speak to God in our depressive state.

When we are depressed, we often withdraw into ourselves, shutting everyone and everything out. That's one option. But it isn't the best one.

We can also allow our depression to draw us nearer to God. In a quiet place, in a world strangely altered by the life changes that have come upon us, we focus on the One who is both outside of ourselves and within us. And we soon realize that is precisely where we must focus in order to heal.

MONKS TO THE RESCUE

The ancient Franciscans understood the opportunities of the valleys, if we would only see them as such. They fashioned a prayer that is still with us today:

May God bless you with discomfort at easy answers, hard hearts, half-truths, and superficial relationships, so that you may live from deep within your heart where God's Spirit dwells.

May God bless you with tears to shed for those who suffer from pain, rejection, starvation, and war, so that you may reach out your hand to comfort them and turn their pain into joy.

And may God bless you with enough foolishness to believe that you can make a difference in this world and in your neighborhood, so that you will courageously try what you don't think you can do, but in Jesus Christ you'll have the strength necessary to do.

May God bless you so that you remember we are all called to continue God's redemptive work of love and healing in God's place, in and through God's name, in God's Spirit, continually creating and breathing new life and grace into everything and everyone we touch.

Faith is living in advance what we will only understand in reverse.

God's ways are certainly not our ways, and all too often before the truth sets you free, it will make you miserable. We dare not conclude that what we are going through lacks the divine touch simply because it entered our life without our permission. Faith is living in advance what we will only understand in reverse.

DARK EYES OR BRIGHT?

Matthew 6:22–23 reminds us that "the eye is the lamp of the body; so then if your eye is clear, your whole body will be full of light. But if your eye is bad, your whole body will be full of darkness. If then the light that is in you is darkness, how great is the darkness!"

We do not see with our eyes. We actually see with our brains. Our eyes are the lenses through which we see. They transfer the image to our occipital lobe in the back of our brains. In conjunction with the frontal lobe, we then define the image as good or bad; we accept it or reject it, and it can bring fear or peace. We choose or decide what definition to give to what we see. The meaning is not always inherent in what we see but *how* we see. Mixed with faith and choice, we can see things as good for us—or bad. We can choose to receive or reject what we see, allow it to make us fearful or bring us peace.

Recently I have been taking riding lessons. At first, the thought of a thousand-pound animal stepping on my toes or bucking me off brought fear and concern, and I'm sure the horse could sense my fear. But as time went on, I came to realize the gentleness of the horse and how well trained it was. My confidence grew and my concerns subsided, and the time spent on horseback displaced the fear I had with a calming effect. What changed? The horse?

No. My eyes.

> **The way we view our problem oftentimes *is* the problem!**

When Jesus talks about our eye, He refers to the way we perceive life's events. If we perceive them poorly and negatively, they will adversely affect us emotionally as well as physically.

Depression isn't necessarily a sin, but we can indeed fall into sin by an inaccurate or distorted perception of God, others, or our circumstances. The way we view our problem oftentimes *is* the problem! If our perception is poor, opportunities become terrifying and invitations appear as threats.

A BIRD'S-EYE VIEW

The fact is, *where you stand will always affect what you see.*

If you're on the observation deck of a skyscraper, you will see the surrounding city—and perhaps the countryside beyond the city, out on the hazy horizon. But if you're standing at the bottom of a ten-foot trench, you won't see anything but dirt, a worm or two, maybe a few rocks, and above you, a narrow strip of sky.

> "What is the difference between an obstacle and an opportunity? Our attitude toward it. Every opportunity has a difficulty, and every difficulty has an opportunity."
>
> **J. SIDLOW BAXTER**

So how do you navigate your way out of this quagmire?

Paul was a man of great confidence even in the midst of storms and snakebites, because he knew God had a divine commission for him.

CONSIDER YOUR CALLING

In the turbulence of depression, when you do not know which way to turn, focus back on what God called you to do in the first place. It's the common denominator of life. Write it on a yellow pad of paper. Discuss it with your spouse. Make it your target. It will give you back a sense of purpose, and hope will start to return.

In Acts 27–28, we read about a storm that attacked the boat carrying Paul the apostle as he was on his way to Rome. The boat crashed and everyone on board had to bail out and swim for their lives. When Paul finally reached dry land, he began gathering sticks for a fire. As he laid his sticks on the fire, a poisonous viper came out and latched onto his arm. Paul simply shook it off and went about his task.

Where did Paul get such confidence to go through storm, shipwreck, and snakebite? Five chapters earlier, the Lord appeared to Paul and said, "Take courage; for as you have solemnly witnessed to My cause at Jerusalem, so you must witness at Rome also" (Acts 23:11 NASB).

> "The grand essentials of happiness are: something to do, something to love, and something to hope for."
>
> **ALLAN K. CHALMERS**

Paul knew his divine commission. When the storm hit, everyone around him was screaming, "We're going to die!" Paul said, "I'm not. I'm going to Rome." When the shipwreck left him stranded, he had confidence that God would rescue him. When the snake threatened him, Paul said, "Don't bother me, I am going to Rome." Paul was a man of great confidence even in the midst of storms and snakebites, because he knew God had a divine commission for him.

I too am under a divine commission. So are you. When storms hit and snakes bite, remind yourself of your high calling.

What has God called you to do? What will He hold you accountable for at the end of your life?

What has God called you to do? What will He hold you accountable for at the end of your life?

Write down the first, second, and third priorities of your calling. Place this list somewhere readily accessible so you can come back to it when needed. When depression hits, look at your divine commission and say, "That is where I need to start again." God will give you hope as you begin to see your potential.

When depression hits, look at your divine commission and say, "That is where I need to start again."

Then, however long it takes, start the rebuilding process. It can take the rest of your life, but you will know that you are on the right track, and nothing, absolutely nothing, will give you the confidence you need like knowing that you are doing His bidding.

REBUILDING

When we see things dimly, we invite depression, which can be defined as a *perceived inability to reconstruct your future.*

Thomas Carlyle wrote *The History of the French Revolution* by hand before computers or even typewriters existed. After three years of writing and lengthy research, he had a fifteen-hundred-page manuscript. He gave his finished work to John Stuart Mills to edit and proofread. Mills put the manuscript in a basket so he could work on it in the evenings by firelight. While he was on a trip, his maid saw the stack of paper and thought it was there to help start the fire. The entire manuscript was destroyed by the time John Stuart Mills returned.

When Thomas Carlyle found out about this, he went into a deep depression. He drew the blinds on his house and refused to eat. After a couple of weeks, he opened one of the blinds. Across the street he saw a man working on a brick wall that had broken down in front of an old church. For three weeks, eight hours a day, Carlyle watched the man rebuild that wall, one brick at a time. When the wall was rebuilt, it looked as good as new.

"If he can rebuild that wall brick by brick," Carlyle said, "I can rebuild my manuscript page by page." He began to write, and within two years he finished it. Today Thomas Carlyle's *The History of the French Revolution* is a classic of historical literature.

If you have lost something valuable, you may have to start all over again. Begin with your original calling. That will give you direction for the rest.

SUFFERING FOR GOOD

The apostle Peter was no stranger to suffering. He writes these words: "Therefore, those also who suffer according to the will of God shall entrust their souls to a faithful Creator in doing what is right" (1 Peter 4:19).

Did you hear that? "Those also who suffer according to the will of God...." There is a way to suffer that is according to the will of God, and there is a way to suffer that is not. The issue isn't the particulars of your suffering but how you perceive it.

It's your choice.

> "The greater [the] difficulty, the more glory in surmounting it. Skillful pilots gain their reputation from storms and tempests."
>
> **EPICURUS**

I had to realize that I was frail, susceptible to failure, and desperately in need of His grace. Until I could change my mind and adjust my perceptions, I could not move out of victim status and begin the climb toward renewed health and joy.

We will all suffer. We have no choice in that matter, but we can choose *what we will suffer for!*

If the purpose of that suffering is to find God's best in my life, I can square my shoulders and accept whatever comes my way!

Until I began to see my depression as a constant reminder that I needed to stay close to God, it was simply an annoying pain that plagued me daily. My first step toward rehabilitation was to see my depression as a positive challenge that drew me closer to Christ on a daily basis.

SEEING IS BELIEVING

> "Believers, look up—take courage. The angels are nearer than you think."
>
> BILLY GRAHAM

You may have heard this story about a man named Michael. Michael is a guy you would really love. He is always in a good mood and always has something positive to say. When someone asks him, "How are you doing, Mike?" he always replies, "If I were doing any better, I'd have to be twins."

If an employee was having a bad day, Michael was right there telling the employee how to look on the positive side of the situation. One day a friend went up to Michael and said, "I don't get it. You can't be that positive all the time."

Michael replied, "Each morning I say to myself, 'Michael, you have two choices today. You can choose to be in a good mood or you can choose to be in a bad mood. I choose to be in a good mood.' Each time something bad happens, I say to myself, 'I can choose to be a victim to this situation and cave in, or I can learn from it and be better. I choose to learn from it and be better.' Every time someone comes complaining, I say to myself, 'I can choose to accept their complaining and be deflated, or I can choose to be positive and grow. I choose to be positive and grow.'"

"Okay," his friend said, "you're right, but it isn't always that easy!"

Mike replied, "Life is all about choices. When you cut away all of the junk, every situation is going to be a choice. You choose how to react to certain situations. You choose to be thankful, or you choose to be worried. You choose to gain God's insight, or

> "A pessimist sees the difficulty in every opportunity; an optimist sees the opportunity in every difficulty."
>
> **WINSTON CHURCHILL**

you choose to be blinded by anger. You choose the life that you will live."

Over the next months, Michael's friend reflected on what Michael had said. He no longer saw him, but often thought about him. Several years later, he heard that Michael had been involved in a serious accident. He had fallen sixty feet from a communications tower. After eighteen hours of surgery and months of intensive care, Michael was released from the hospital with rods in his back.

Michael's friend saw him a few years after the accident and asked him, "How are you?"

"If I were any better," he replied, "I'd have to be twins. Do you want to see my scars?"

He declined, but he did ask, "What went through your mind, Michael, when that accident took place?"

"As I lay there on the ground," he told me, "I remembered I had two choices. I could choose to live or I could choose to die. I chose to live."

"Weren't you scared?"

"Yes, but the paramedics were great. They kept telling me that I was going to be fine. But when they wheeled me into the emergency room, I saw the expressions on the faces of the doctors. Then I got really scared. Their eyes said, 'This one is a dead man.' When I saw that, I knew I needed to take action."

"So what did you do?"

"Well," he said, "You know, those nurses shout out questions to you even though you're in pain."

"Yes, I know."

"Well, the nurse asked me, 'Are you allergic to anything?'

"'Yes,' I replied, 'I am.'

"The doctors and nurses abruptly stopped working on me. They said, 'You are? What are you allergic to?'

"'Gravity,' I said. Over their laughter, I told them, 'Listen, I am choosing to live. So operate on me as if you are operating on a man who is alive, not on a man who is dead.'"

Michael lived, thanks not only to the skill of his doctor but also because of his choice to live. The same choice is extended to us every single day—choose to live.

Choose to live. Living well must become intentional.

Living well must become intentional. Don't stop dreaming of what your life can yet be . . . without the fishtailing, without the excess, but with all the fruitfulness. You may never become all that you dream of, but you'll never achieve anything that you don't dream of.

What choice will you make?

———

Reflections

Dr. Wayne, I just had to send you this letter to thank you for saving my life.

I lead a church in a small coastal town in South Africa. Lately I would just start crying for no reason. I felt like a failure, and I considered leaving the ministry. Worst of all was that I didn't understand what was happening or why. I felt depressed and was thinking of asking my wife for a divorce.

Last week a pastor friend of mine gave me a DVD with one of your presentations from a leadership summit you spoke at. As I watched it, I could identify with everything you said. I immediately went to see my doctor and he confirmed everything you mentioned. He immediately sat me down and worked out a plan of restoration and healing. Finally I understood what was going on with me. I realize it's only the beginning and that I still have a long way to go.

But God used you to save my life, my marriage, my home, and my ministry. Thank you so much!

—PASTOR FROM SOUTH AFRICA

Chapter Eight
Seven Lessons
Hard-Learned

"A wise man will hear and increase in learning, and a man of understanding will acquire wise counsel."

PROVERBS 1:5

I knew that I had to restructure my life. There was no other option. Healing from the anxiety was where I would begin, but restructuring the way I lived would keep me for the long haul. I realized that what had fueled my engine in the beginning, if not adjusted, would destroy me in the end.

I had to revisit my motivations and everything that had brought me to this point. The battle would be overcoming the habits and subconscious patterns that were so deeply embedded in my soul. I had to recognize the triggers that had contributed to this distressing mental state and change them.

"Those things that hurt, instruct."

BENJAMIN FRANKLIN

I had emerged from the deep forest, but I was not yet out of the woods. I was out of my emotional ICU, but I noticed that slight mishaps in relationships, overcrowded schedules, and unexpected demands sucked me back—at least temporarily—into depression.

BEWARE OF RELAPSE

There is one thing you must learn about burnout: From now on, depression will never be far away. You may not be feeling your way along a dark forest pathway, but the woods will never be completely out of view. String a few failures together, or have a problem at home, and you may very well feel the shadows begin to blot out your view of the sun once again. You may find yourself withdrawing, searching for repose and solitude.

When that happens, find it. Take it. Pull the plug for a while, even if it's only for a day.

> "The only real mistake is the one from which we learn nothing."
>
> **JOHN POWELL**

The leader who is running on empty has just enough energy to sustain himself for the next step; the emotional reserves are thin. He must know how to keep his stride and not deplete his resources. To do so once is a lesson hard-learned. To repeat it again is just plain dumb.

Those who have come through burnout will live along the border for a few years, and your awareness of this one fact can save you from being caught again. You have escaped the prison of depression, but you're not home yet. Be wise; live differently, but don't get overconfident. I made that mistake and was not ready for life's twists and turns.

A year after the burnout, I was feeling my oats again. I guess I kicked into high gear when we faced some staffing problems, and I knew I had to jump in and correct the ship before it hit a reef. I'm a problem solver, so this stoked my jets.

I felt invincibility returning, and I ran hard for two months. I loved the feeling. I consumed several cups of high-octane caffeine each morning to keep my energy level up. I compromised on my exercise because I felt strong and energetic. I couldn't wait to get up in the morning. I was back. I was bulletproof again!

Or so I thought.

Be wise; live differently, but don't get overconfident.

Then the erratic heartbeats returned, and one day I found myself struggling to get my breath. I knew I was headed for trouble. Immediately clearing my schedule, I took several days off with my wife. I headed for a neighboring island, and the first day I collapsed—ill and exhausted. Each succeeding day I found myself returning to normal, but my normal had to be redefined. My default system had to be reprogrammed.

Here are seven lessons that grew out of that frightening relapse. These suggestions will help to get your resilience awakened and your engine running in the right direction.

LESSON ONE: DO NOT OVERPRODUCE

I have always been an overachiever, even before I came to Christ. And when I did, I simply gave those efforts to God. I didn't change the fuels. It was still me working hard for God.

I don't often relate my dreams to people. I've heard enough strange ones by well-meaning Christians to discount dream interpretation altogether. But this one was vivid—with a lesson that has never left my soul.

Come Back Tomorrow

Nearing the time of a possible second burnout, I had a poignant dream of a man and his family who ran a small farm. In this dream, people were buying various products: one bought a gallon of milk, another ripe tomatoes, another cheese, others eggs or corn.

A lady came and asked for something they didn't have, but the farmer simply said, *"Come back tomorrow and I'll have more."* The irate woman gave the farmer a sour look, but it didn't bother him. He just went back to work. That was how it was on the farm. The chickens can lay only so many eggs a day, cows have just so much fresh milk, and a few more tomatoes will ripen tomorrow.

> **When the clock runs out, then I say, "Come back tomorrow, and I'll have more."**

Yet people still came, standing in line for the products, buying up everything until the farmer sold out for the day. This happened every day because this particular farm's goods were the freshest and finest anywhere. And when they ran out (as they inevitably did), the farmer would say, *"Come back tomorrow and I'll have more."*

I woke up from that dream with a new view of life and ministry. I don't have to tie myself to an imaginary, unrelenting cycle to produce more, make more, or try to outdo last week's numbers. I have just so much time in the day, and I want to do what I can with all my heart involved. When the clock runs out, then I say, "Come back tomorrow, and I'll have more."

In other words, I don't want to kill myself by overproducing or doing anything without the quality that God and His people deserve. And I also want to leave time to recharge. So I had to establish some guardrails and make some restrictions in my life. The only one who can do that in your life is you! It is not a board decision or your response to a spouse's complaints. It has to be you!

LESSON TWO: STEWARD YOUR ENERGY

A leader's greatest asset is not necessarily time. It is *energy*. A person with energy can accomplish more in four hours than another would in four days. With energy, a father can share in an activity with his son or daughter with huge and lingering memories that simply spending time with them would never accomplish.

I know—I've read the books too that say, "Love is spelled T-I-M-E." But allow me to challenge that thinking for a moment.

I had gone through numerous evolutions in my understanding of this crucial concept until one evening, over dinner in Jakarta, Indonesia, I came to a clear understanding. Bill Hybels and I were discussing my next season of life, and he began talking about investing my life energies *strategically*—into arenas of catalytic importance. Only by intentional investments, he explained, will the outlay of my energy expenditures reach beyond my initial contributions.

I don't remember what Bill and I had for dinner that night, but I do remember the dominant thought that I took back with me to my hotel room. I realized that *I had to invest my bursts of energy more intentionally, and in doing so, I would be able to extend my ministry shelf life.*

Vegging in the same office we have been hanging out in for the past umpteen years may not be the path to productivity. The passing of time will make us old, but it won't guarantee that we will become fruitful.

"Well," some say, "God won't grade us on results, He will only grade on faithfulness." Really? And is it faithful to squander our precious stores of God-given energy in a go-nowhere circumstance that neither challenges our hearts nor quickens our hunger for life?

I had to invest my bursts of energy more intentionally.

I have witnessed many who have been at a job or a ministry for an extended number of years, but the fruit is small and anemic. Conversely, I have seen others who in a short amount of time have cultivated expansive orchards, bearing wholesome produce and abundant harvests. The difference? Not just time but . . .

Energy.

Each of us has a finite amount of energy to invest each day, and how we invest that will make all the difference.

Maybe at one time in my foolish youth I was an energy dynamo throwing off a constant flow over hours, days, and even weeks. Now I measure my energy in bursts or pockets of energy. I have found that I have about *seven bursts* of energy each day that I can invest. I must choose wisely where and when to invest these pockets of life vitality, because (as the used-car dealer says on the TV ads) when they're gone, they're gone.

And when they're gone, I'm useless.

How and where I invest my energy may be the most important decision I will make on any given day. If I'm not careful and judicious, my energy stores will be squandered on e-mail and useless activities. Consistently mis-investing energy will bring about a level of exhaustion that will plague me like a low-grade fever.

Here is how I seek to assign my seven pockets of daily energy. Your list, of course, will be different from mine, depending on your calling and place in life. But regardless of the variances, you can see that the investment of energy must be specific and targeted. The principle is applicable and transferable.

I will give the first and best part of my day to sitting at His feet.

Number One Is in My Daily Devotions

As I did early this morning, I will give the first and best part of my day to sitting at His feet. As the old hymn says, "I come to the garden alone, while the dew is still on the roses." As I explain in my book *The Divine Mentor*, I follow a reading program that takes me through the Old Testament once and the New Testament twice each year. I then journal my thoughts using the acrostic SOAP. (Scripture, Observation, Application, Prayer), gaining a gem of wisdom that the Holy Spirit knows I will require that day.

The Second Pocket of Energy I Give to Message Preparation

I do this a little each day. I cannot put off message preparation until Saturday. I must intentionally invest some energy toward it every day.

The Next Three Pockets of Energy I Give Toward the Ministry of Pastoring and Leading

When it comes to my ministry day, I ask myself,

- What areas of my life and ministry could most benefit from an infusion of my energy?
- Which areas will be catalytic and advance the kingdom?

- What groups of people do I need to energize and inspire?

- What growth areas require my involvement?

- Which aspects of ministry by my involvement will result in growth and fruitfulness?

- What is it around New Hope that needs a burst of my energy to release it or unclog it?

- Where am I going to assign my pockets of energy that will in fact take the ministry to a new level?

I Have Found That I Need to Reserve the Sixth Pocket of Energy for My Marriage and My Family

If I use everything up at the office, I come home depleted and have nothing left for my loved ones at home.

In a relay race, the baton isn't transferred when the lead runner is staggering and exhausted. He is at the top of his stride when he reaches the other runner in the box.

Your family is the other runner in the box. They need you at full stride. Many ministry leaders make contact with their families when they are at the lowest point of their stride . . . when they're stumbling with mindless exhaustion. Is it any wonder why so many ministers' families are on the slow slide south?

> "Succeeding in business and failing at home is a cop-out. For no success in the workplace will ever make up for failure at home."
>
> HOWARD HENDRICKS

Last but Not Necessarily Least, I Reserve One Final Pocket of Energy for Me

I need to exercise. If I stop exercising, then all of the rest of my energy priorities will soon be in the tank. And the fact is, if I am already used up when I leave the office, I won't want to exercise. I'll want to flop into an easy chair or stretch out on the floor. With my mind exhausted and my energy spent, a nice dinner in front of the TV will seem like the most logical choice for an evening activity.

If you do not steward your energy, a few years and fifteen pounds later you will realize that you borrowed all the available pockets of energy you had and invested them in your job, career, or ministry. You gave what was left over (if any) to what was most important. You let the home fires grow cold, you threw leftover bones toward God, and you neglected your body, hoping against hope that the diet pills would do the rest. You will face a famine—at home, in your disposition, and in your soul.

> "Energy and persistence conquer all things."
>
> **BENJAMIN FRANKLIN**

Like it or not, you will be poised for clogs in your relationships, in your soul, and in your arteries. You will sense it, and the ragged edges of life will confirm the slow, downward spiral. You will begin to see "mini-strokes" in your relationship with your spouse, your children will show signs of straying, and your relationship with God will have lost its vibrancy.

Steward your energy well, and in seasons of dismay, you will still have enough of a reservoir to lead.

When the pain is sufficient, and hopefully the time is not too late, you will need to borrow all you can from your ministry in order to make up for the famine in your relationship with God, your family, and your health. If you don't, you may face a breakdown, an affair, or a divorce.

Steward your energy well, and in seasons of dismay, you will still have enough of a reservoir to lead.

LESSON THREE: REST WELL, MY FRIEND

We are never more vulnerable to depression from burnout than when we are totally fatigued and overtired. Even Jesus, when He felt weary and overwhelmed, said to His disciples, "Come away . . . and rest a while" (see Mark 6:31). One of the very first steps in reversing depression and regaining a sense of resilience is rest. Increase your rest until you begin to feel some semblance of renewal, even if it begins with small doses.

> **We are never more vulnerable to depression than when we are totally fatigued or overtired.**

Every person may require varying amounts of rest for different seasons. Begin by not setting an alarm clock and observe your sleep patterns. If you wake too often in the night, resolve that first. Earplugs, warm milk, or even sleep aids in controlled amounts will help you begin the healing process. Sleep requirements cannot be ignored. Your body as well as your psyche is demanding rest, and you need to attend to those needs.

Be still, and know that I am God. (Psalm 46:10 NIV)

I came across a contemporary version of the twenty-third Psalm entitled "Psalm 23 Revisited." In it, the author captures perfectly where many of us are today:

> The clock is my dictator, I shall not rest.
> It makes me lie down only when exhausted.
> It leads me into deep depression, it hounds my soul.
> It leads me in circles of frenzy for activities' sake.
> Even though I run frantically from task to task,
> I will never get it all done, for my "ideal" is with me.
> Deadlines and my need for approval, they drive me.

They demand performance from me, beyond the limits of
my schedule.
They anoint my head with migraines, my in-basket
overflows.
Surely fatigue and time pressure shall follow me all the
days of my life.
And I will dwell in the bonds of frustration forever.[1]

Composers know the importance of scoring into each piece
appropriate rests. And legatos, or longer-held notes, can make an
otherwise rough piece of music smooth. They invite the strings
to sing and the woodwinds to echo. Noah benShea, in *Jacob the
Baker*, writes: "It's the space between the notes that makes the
music."

I have learned the importance of this truth in my life song. I
must write in the rests before the conductor collapses from the
continuous staccatos, detached notes incessantly fired in rapid
succession. I need longer notes. I needed more *legatos* . . . with
feeling. I needed to take time to enjoy
the day, the moment, the present, before
rushing into the next.

Legatos—life will not be rushed.

But finding those legatos doesn't
always come easily.

> "It's the space between
> the notes that makes
> the music."
>
> **NOAH BENSHEA**

Unlearning

As I mentioned earlier, my father was a first sergeant in the
army. Translated, that meant whenever I rested, I was seen as *lazy*.
His work ethic came from his immigrant family, and their labor
knew no bounds. So over the years I developed a complex . . .
whenever I took a break, I felt guilty.

Unable to conquer the habit, I used to fill my calendar with
appointments, and if there was some space left over, I'd take a
break. This worked in theory, but more often than not those

"spaces" got filled with unexpected funerals, family needs, urgent marriage counseling requests, and kids' activities.

Even when I knew I couldn't keep up the pace, that I was headed for a breakdown, I booked more and more speaking engagements and leadership seminars so I wouldn't struggle with feelings of guilt. I was never able to unhook from the apparatus of ministry, even though I was "on vacation."

Life will not be rushed.

Drink . . . Don't Drive

I remember training for a long-distance race. My coach instructed me to hydrate at certain time intervals. "Every fifteen minutes," he told me, "you drink six ounces of water. Keep an eye on your watch so you don't violate your hydration limits."

"But, Coach, what if I am not thirsty?"

"Listen to me, Cordeiro. *If you wait until you're thirsty to take a drink, it's too late.* Your body is already into dehydration. You can't afford that."

One of the greatest lessons I'm learning (and yes, I am *still* learning it) is that rest is not sin. Taking a break doesn't mean you're lazy or that you're not as valuable. Catching your breath now and then doesn't mean you're not carrying your load, or that you are somehow less than committed to your church, your company, or your calling.

It was (and is) a hard-learned lesson.

Another benefit of scheduling in breaks at regular intervals is that my wife is much happier. In an extraordinarily busy season, she can look at the calendar and know there's light at the end of the tunnel. It has also helped me in the process of planning out my year. Knowing in advance where my breaks are, I can make plans to book guest speakers at the church or wrap up project deadlines.

If you wait until you're thirsty to take a drink, it's too late. Your body is already into dehydration.

Schedule rests in *before* your calendar fills up. Rest is not an afterthought; it has to be a primary *responsibility*. It brings a rhythm back to life and a cadence that makes life sustainable. If you are tired, your soul gets weary. And if your soul gets weary, you've depleted more than you can afford.

When I was younger (I find myself saying that more these days), I could run till exhausted and be revived within the hour. Not anymore. I would heal with speed. I could cut my leg off in the morning, and no problem—I'd grow another by noon.

Not anymore.

God gives us rest, but sometimes we can't seem to accept such an extravagant gift. We somehow imagine that the world won't be able to go on without our involvement. There's too much to do. Yet God says: "You shall do no work at all. . . . It is to be a sabbath of complete rest to you, and you shall humble your souls" (Leviticus 23:31–32).

"Humble your souls"?

What does that mean? God is saying that if we wait until the work is done before we rest, we will never rest. The work will *never* be done! So even in the midst of the work, we have to cease and rest.

Why? *Do you mean to tell me I'm not indispensable?*

This may be a really rude awakening, but the fact is, the world will go on even if we are not involved for a day. Don't think about this one too long, but the world will also go on even after we depart this life. I know it's difficult to contemplate, but it is true. When we rest at predesignated intervals, we are reminding ourselves that ultimately God controls the outcomes, not me or all of my wonderful efforts. It's good for us to wean ourselves off the need to be needed. For many of us, that will be the beginning of health.

Rest has to be a primary *responsibility*. It brings a rhythm back to life and a cadence that makes life sustainable.

If we violate the Sabbath rest, something morphs in our soul. We start to get proud, edgy, anxious.

The psalmist tells us, "It is vain for you to rise up early, to retire late, to eat the bread of painful labors; for He gives to His beloved even in his sleep" (Psalm 127:2).

God Humbles Our Souls on a Sabbath

I recall when this truth was truly brought home to me. We were living in Eugene, Oregon, before Anna and I moved home to Hawaii. I had a full schedule of two weeks of speaking engagements down in California. One of them was a very large and prestigious men's camp, and I was the keynote speaker.

> "The mark of a successful man is one that has spent an entire day on the bank of a river without feeling guilty about it."
>
> **AUTHOR UNKNOWN**

I had been in a long season of not taking any Sabbaths, burning the candle at both ends, and going about eighty miles an hour. As I was gearing up to this full two-week schedule, I started to get sicker and sicker.

Finally, I had to go to the doctor. I asked him to just give me something so I could do everything I needed to do. He examined me and said, "I'm sorry, Wayne, you can't go anywhere."

"Why not?" I asked.

He said, "Because you have double pneumonia. It's in both lungs."

I said, "Just give me something—like a shot—so I can go!"

"No," he said. "If you don't rest, you will die!"

I went home depressed. I was so sick I could not get out of bed the next morning. When I stubbornly attempted to, the room began spinning. I fell back onto the mattress and stayed put for two weeks. My wife canceled my scheduled speaking engagements. I felt upset and embarrassed—especially because I had made several commitments that I felt I couldn't back out of. One was that men's camp. Surely I had ruined it!

Being in bed for two weeks bothered me, but what bothered me more was when I called the director of the men's camp two weeks later to again apologize. His voice was so . . . well, cheerful. "No problem, Wayne. We found another speaker at the last minute, and he did a great job! God moved in such a mighty way that we are thinking about having him back again next year!"

"*God* can't *move*," I thought. "*I wasn't there! Don't tell me God moved in a great way!*"

God does, and He will. God says, "Let me humble your soul with rest. It's not all about *you*. I can get the work done."

Do you mean to tell me I'm not indispensable?

When we rest, God continues His work. When we reenter, it is with a humbled soul, hungry again for what He has called us to do. We return once again as a servant.

Letting Our Souls Catch Up

A man went on safari in an exotic country, hiring some local guides to manage his procession. Because he had arrived late, he was already three days behind schedule, and the original safari had left without him. So the hired men sprinted to catch up.

After the first day of running in the jungle heat, the men fell exhausted at the evening campfire. Early the next morning, the visitor blew his whistle: "Come on! Let's go! Let's catch that safari!" The men jumped up, strapped on the bags, and started running.

Long after the sun had set, they finally stopped, once again falling in sheer exhaustion. The foreigner was well-pleased, saying, "If we keep up this pace, we may catch the others!" So the next morning, they got up in a hurry and ran again—all day long.

On the fourth day, the eager visitor sprung to his feet and exclaimed, "Today we shall surely catch them! Let's go!"

But the hired men just sat around the dying fire, poking the embers with sticks. "Get moving right now!" urged the man.

The leader of the men replied, "We're not moving."

Indignant, the foreigner insisted, "I paid you to help me catch up with the safari!"

"Sir," said the leader with a firm calmness, "we are not going to move all day. You have pushed us so hard these first three days. Now we will have to wait a whole day . . . to let our souls catch up!"

Lead out of rest and allow your soul to catch up to you.

Lead out of rest and allow your soul to catch up to you. Only then will you be able to put your heart into everything God asks of you. Without rest, you are leading on empty.

Sleep In Right

When does your day begin? When do you start your day? A typical answer is, "Whenever I wake up, of course!"

On the contrary, let's take a look at the creation story. In Genesis, when God created the days, we find these words: "So the evening and the morning were the first day" (Genesis 1:5 NKJV). This pattern is repeated as God continues to create on each successive day.

"So the evening and the morning were the second day" (Genesis 1:8 NKJV).

Learn to sleep in on the front side of the clock.

In other words, God started each day in the evening, not the morning. Your day does not begin when you get up. It starts when you go to sleep. Rest begins your new day, not coffee.

For years I had it wrong. I thought my day began with the morning's activity, but instead, it actually began with the evening's rest. I had to reprogram my mind to that biblical reality. The success of any short race is determined at the start, and now that my days are getting shorter (or at least it seems that way!) I need to start better—in the evenings.

There are two ways to win a race. One is to be faster than everyone else, and the other is to start sooner! In a normal race, that's called cheating. But in life, it's called *wisdom*. For an Olympian, it is called illegal. For a Christian, it is called *biblical*.

If you ever need to sleep in, learn to sleep in on the front side of the clock, not the back side. Simply said, your deepest sleep is when your REM cycles happen, and that typically takes place between 11 PM and 3 AM. That is when you will get your deepest sleep. If you miss getting to bed before 1 AM, you will have missed half your chance at receiving your deepest rest. You may think you can sleep in until 9 AM to get your eight hours of sleep. But you are mistaken! You will have had the sleep time, but not the rest. Your sleep will be shallow compared to what it could have been, and when you awaken just before noon, you'll still feel sluggish and lethargic.

So what I say is this: "You can sleep in on the back side dumb, or sleep in on the front side smart." Go to bed at 8 PM and get up at 5 AM. Then you will have had nine hours of sleep! I wake up every day at 5 AM, and people say, "You're up early!" Actually, I just slept in! I feel much better. I am ready for my day. I am much healthier when I cooperate with God's design for my body.

Learn to sleep in on the front side of the clock. Sleep right and double your rest.

LESSON FOUR: EXERCISE YOUR WAY TO RECOVERY

If you're depressed, you may feel constantly exhausted, so putting on your sneakers and going to the gym could seem like the least important thing on your list. But it's a fact: Exercise is important for both your physical and mental health.

Varying studies from different sources all reveal the same finding: A balanced regimen of physical activity can help with recovery from depression. One such study showed that exercise— three sessions of aerobic activity each week—worked about as well as medication when it came to reducing the symptoms of depression. In addition, research concluded that after one year, people who exercised were much less likely to relapse than people who took medicine. The results were published in the journal *Psychosomatic Medicine* in 2000. A 2005 study in the *American Journal of Preventive Medicine* showed that moderate aerobic workouts, done three to five times weekly, cut mild to moderate depression symptoms nearly in half.

Regular exercise has been proven to:

- Reduce stress, anxiety, and depression
- Boost your sagging self-esteem
- Bring a sense of well-being
- Produce a brighter outlook on life
- Improve sleep

Start small, but start NOW!

Exercise also has these other health benefits:

- Strengthens the heart
- Makes the body better able to use oxygen
- Builds energy levels
- Lowers blood pressure
- Improves muscle tone and strength
- Helps reduce body fat
- Makes you look fit and healthy and feel better about yourself

Here are some tips for starting off a new exercise routine.

Start Small

Don't jump from months of television watching (where the only exercise you had was pressing the remote control button) to marathon training! That will just leave you frustrated, in pain, and demoralized. Here's how I say it: "Start small, but start NOW!" Don't procrastinate until you feel ready or until you're in shape. The only way to get into shape is to exercise. So instead of signing up for the city's next annual marathon, gradually work your way up. Start by exercising for a short period of time—a few minutes or more—only on a few days of the week. Don't do more than that for a week or two. Slowly build up to exercising for half an hour or more, four days a week. Too much vigorous exercise can cause the body to go into survival mode and upset its delicate balance. This is why it is vital to begin exercise gradually and increase it gradually.

Break It Up

You don't have to get all of your physical activity in a single stretch or with one activity. Many people prefer doing smaller sessions of exercise during the day and varying the types of exercise. Three fifteen-minute walks are as good as one forty-five-minute walk. Don't push yourself over the edge. Smaller chunks spaced out are much better than working out hard one day and expecting to wake up Superman the next morning. It won't happen.

Try different types of physical activity until you find one that you really enjoy!

Pick Something You Enjoy

This advice may seem obvious. But a lot of people choose a sport not because they like it, but because they think that it will be good for them. If you treat exercise like a bitter medicine—distasteful but good for your health—you probably won't stick with it. Remember that there are a lot of activities to choose from, and they can be enjoyable. I paddle a one-man canoe not primarily because it is good for my health, but rather because I enjoy the sport. I love riding waves in the ocean, and before I realize it, I have had a two-hour aerobic exercise that has replenished my soul. Go for a hike, ride a horse, or take a fun exercise class. Try different types of physical activity until you find one that you really enjoy!

Exercise With Friends

Solo physical activity is sometimes hard to maintain unless you are extremely disciplined, but if you exercise with someone else, you might feel more committed. Find an exercise partner. Make a date to walk with your spouse or friend at a specific time, on specific days. For a season, my wife, Anna, played a regular tennis game with friends. Many people find that structured classes like aerobics help them stick with a program.

Make It an Everyday Activity

Try adding a little extra physical activity whenever and wherever you can during your daily routine. Take the stairs rather than the elevator. Park a little farther away so you can sneak in a little extra walking. Walk to the post office that's a few blocks away and save gasoline. (That option is becoming more of a necessity these days!) Over time, little changes to your behavior can add up to a big improvement in your health and a move away from depression and isolation.

Research has shown that physical exercise is one of the best tension relievers. Nothing eases stress more than exercise, and when appropriately carried out, it helps you to function at peak efficiency.

LESSON FIVE: EATING YOUR WAY TO A GOOD LIFE

Often it takes a brush with death to get us to rearrange our diet and opt for better nutrition. Don't wait for that to happen. While there is no specific food group that will guarantee the reduction of depression (sorry, chocolate lovers), improving your diet and eating habits can help as part of an overall treatment for depression. There's more and more research indicating that, in many ways, food and mood are intricately connected.

Dietary changes can bring about chemical as well as physiological changes. These changes can improve mood and mental outlook. Here are four tips for eating your way back to health.

1. Eat Foods That Are High in Nutrients

Nutrients in foods support the body's repair, growth, and wellness. Steer clear of fast food, empty foods like potato chips and Twinkies, and snack on vegetable sticks instead. Go green as often as you can with at least 60 percent of your diet in raw foods, such as fruits and vegetables.

2. Fill Your Plate With Delicious Antioxidants

Damaging molecules called free radicals are produced in our bodies during normal body functions—and these free radicals contribute to aging and dysfunction. Studies show that the brain is particularly at risk for free radical damage. Antioxidants such as beta-carotene and vitamins C and E combat the effects of free radicals.

Sources of beta-carotene: apricots, broccoli, cantaloupe, carrots, collards, peaches, pumpkin, spinach, and sweet potatoes.

Eat your way back to health.

Sources of vitamin C: blueberries, broccoli, grapefruit, kiwi, oranges, peppers, potatoes, strawberries, and tomatoes.

Sources of vitamin E: margarine, nuts and seeds, vegetable oils, wheat germ.

3. The Calming Effect of "Smart Carbs"

The connection between carbohydrates and mood is linked to the mood-boosting brain chemical serotonin. Adding moderate amounts of foods high in carbohydrates (breads, cereal, pasta) raises the level of serotonin in the brain. When serotonin levels rise, we feel a calming effect, less anxiety, and a whole lot better about life.

4. Eat Protein-Rich Foods to Boost Alertness

Foods rich in protein, like turkey, tuna, or chicken, are rich in an amino acid called tyrosine. Tyrosine boosts levels of the brain chemical dopamine. This boost helps you feel alert and makes it easier to concentrate. Some good sources of protein foods that boost alertness are beans and peas, lean beef, low-fat cheese, fish, milk, poultry, soy products, and yogurt.

LESSON SIX: RECHARGE DAILY

Solomon wrote, "Watch over your heart with all diligence, for from it flow the springs of life" (Proverbs 4:23). The springs of life! The headwaters of the soul. You can't refresh those springs from the outside in. Only God, the Creator and Sustainer of life, can release those vital energies from deep within the human spirit. There He evaluates, renews, and recharges. It must begin at the headwaters of our souls.

Clear at the Source

Many years ago, as a youth pastor, the highlight of my year was summer camp. But we roughed it in those days. No pristine wilderness cabins with cooks, beautiful chapels, or individual bathrooms. We went to a state camp with three-sided cabins and bunk boards (not bunk beds); you brought your own sleeping mat if you wanted a little cushion between you and the wooden planks.

Our water came from a nearby spring that gave way to a small stream that entered the park. The headwaters of that spring was somewhere in the wilderness that was unknown to us. We were just grateful for the water that we could draw for drinking and cooking.

Each week a state ranger would arrive to test the potability of the water. He usually came and left unnoticed, but not this day. Finding me with a few kids, he said, "Don't drink the water until I come back." Like Mary at the annunciation, I was perplexed by such a greeting. "What's the problem?" I asked. "We've been drinking it for the past two days." He continued, "Well, don't drink any more. The bacteria level is too high. I'm going to check it out." He donned his rubber boots, grabbed a shovel, and disappeared.

I'm sure my stomach began to gurgle at that point, and I made sure I stayed close to the rest rooms until he returned.

Several hours later he entered our campsite. "Okay, you can drink the water now!"

My goal is not to study the Bible for an hour each morning. Rather, it is to let the Bible study me!

"Would you mind telling me why we couldn't drink it?" The ranger reported to me that the bacteria level signaled that something was wrong, and indeed there was. He found a dead deer near the water source, and having been there for a couple of weeks, it was beginning to decompose.

I knew I had to use the rest room then!

When there is something out of place at the headwaters, everything else is affected. We could have tried boiling the water, filtering it, or masking it, but the only way to rectify the problem was to ensure that the source was clear.

In my life, daily devotions do that in a huge way. My goal is not to study the Bible for an hour each morning. Rather, it is to let the Bible study me! David sang in Psalm 139:23–24, "Search me, O God, and know my heart; try me and know my anxious thoughts; and see if there be any hurtful way in me." David was inviting the Lord to evaluate his motives and see if there was anything depleting his soul and subsequently leaching into his life.

There is no recharging like the recharging of God's Spirit that (as one mouthwash commercial used to say) "cleans and refreshes." He renews me in the inmost depths of my being. *Nothing* compares. A vacation at an exotic resort could be relaxing . . . a night at a play on Broadway or a seat at an NFL playoff game could be entertaining . . . a lecture by a celebrated author could be intellectually stimulating . . . a good workout playing your favorite sport could give you that tired-but-rejuvenated feeling for the rest of the day. But it all pales compared to what God can do to refresh and recharge your spirit.

As He fills and refills my inner tank, I am able to reserve adequate time and energy for my family and enjoy my life with my wife, Anna.

Start Fresh Every Morning

Sleep opens a new day for us, a fresh, God-given chance at life. God knew that His creation needed new beginnings. If we didn't, He would have given us our lifetime in one fell swoop. But instead, knowing our needs, He broke our lifetime into bite-sized chunks that we call years, where every 365 days or so everything begins anew. And within that, He gave us four seasons, or quarters, as opportunities to start all over again. Even within that, He factored in what we call months, repetitions of the lunar cycle. And if that weren't enough, He broke each month into days, or twenty-four-hour segments of time, and those into minutes, unlimited opportunities to start again, to begin afresh.

> "Every tomorrow has two handles. We can take hold of it with the handle of anxiety or the handle of faith."
>
> **HENRY WARD BEECHER**

Lamentations 3:22–23 reminds us of this new beginning: "The Lord's loving-kindnesses indeed never cease, for His compassions never fail. *They are new every morning;* great is Your faithfulness" (emphasis added).

We need new beginnings, don't we? God built that longing into us. I have to let yesterday be done with, the joys as well as the sorrows, the trophies and tragedies, and leave them in His hands. They are no longer mine to possess. I cannot cruise through today on yesterday's awards and old press clippings, and neither can I allow past sorrows to dictate a yet uncharted future. New beginnings allow me to tap into fresh potential.

Just a few weeks ago, Anna and I were playing golf when I hit a killer drive. I smacked that ball, and all of a sudden, it was like the wind took it. Airborne and soaring, it took a sharp rightward hook, sailed over two houses, and got lost somewhere in the lava.

I thought, *Oh no,* because that's a two-stroke penalty. Two strokes tacked onto an already crowded scorecard—along with an extra word muttered under my breath. My wife turned to me and said, "Honey, just take a mulligan." A mulligan is a free do-over, no penalty.

I looked at her and thought, *This is why I married this woman.*

Wouldn't it be nice if we could imagine a conversation like this one at the end of the day?

"O God, I don't even know what to say. I messed up so much today."
And the Lord smiles and says, *"Take a mulligan. Just do it over. Tomorrow is your second try, so get some rest."*

> "Whatever the struggle, continue the climb. It may be only one step to the summit."
>
> **DIANE WESTLAKE**

In essence, that is exactly what He does. I'm not saying that we should minimize our sins or deny our problems and mistakes. We need to deal with them correctly, in the way God would have us deal with them. Often we do, but then we still don't take the mulligan!

The Lord says, "I'm giving you forgiveness. Let's start all over."

And we say, "Ah, no, no. I feel so bad. I've got to beat myself to death."

And the Lord says, "Won't you just take it?"

Each and every new day, God gives us another chance. How many of us would say, "Boy, I could really use a new chance at life." This is why God gives us life in twenty-four-hour increments! Each of these time periods is broken with something called rest that rejuvenates us, offering us a fresh perspective and a new beginning.

As David put it, "Weeping may last for the night, but a shout of joy comes in the morning" (Psalm 30:5).

Ralph Waldo Emerson said, "Finish each day and be done with it. You have done what you could; some blunders and absurdities have crept in; forget them as soon as you can. Tomorrow is a new day; you shall begin it serenely and with too high a spirit to be encumbered with your old nonsense."

LESSON SEVEN: FIGHT FOR YOUR FAMILY

Someone once said that the darkest place of any lighthouse is always at its base. The same can be said of our families. A pastor or Christian leader can shine a radiant beam out to the horizons, warning passing ships of dangerous waters . . . while their own unmaintained plumbing floods the home.

Part of my "five percent" is the health and closeness of my family.

And so it is for you, my friend. *Fight for it.* Fight as fiercely as Nehemiah urged his countrymen to fight when the enemies of God and Israel sought to destroy the work of rebuilding the nation. That courageous governor wrote in his journal: "When I saw their fear, I rose and spoke to the nobles, the officials and the rest of the people: 'Do not be afraid of them; remember the Lord who is great and awesome, and fight for your brothers, your sons, your daughters, your wives and your houses'" (Nehemiah 4:14).

Fight for your family. If you miss building that home base, you will have nowhere to go when your ministry days are over.

One day after years of ministry with a wonderful congregation, I will say my good-byes, pack my bags and, with many tears, walk out of the church. But when I walk out of the church, there's only one place I can walk into.

Family.

If you miss building that home base, you will have nowhere to go when your ministry days are over. You'll arrive back on your doorstep with your boxes of books and notes, and you'll have nothing to walk into—except shards of yesterday's mistake of putting your job, ministry, or career ahead of everything else. Restore the preeminence of the family early on. Too many have sacrificed marital harmony and family on the altar of success. It's not worth it.

Here's a fact. Not a judgment, mind you. Just a fact of life. While everyone in our great church loves the Cordeiro family, I have come to realize that nobody is *fighting* for my family. That's my job. That's the task God has given to me. Others may fight for pieces of my time and energy, but no one will fight for my family.

My greatest ministry will be in the *next* generation. And it must carry on into the generation of my grandchildren. I am not done yet!

Although I have two daughters in the Northwest and a son in Hawaii, we stay very dialed-in as a family. There's hardly a day that goes by wherein Anna or I do not communicate with all three of them. Maintaining healthy relationships within my family is a full-time job! It's relentless, but it's worth it. I keep in touch with them not because my children have wayward tendencies. It is simply the natural drift that families are predisposed to. Our modern culture and societal norms introduce a relational slippage. Imperceptibly over time, it can devolve into the Cordeiro *Diaspora* (or the eventual scattering of what was once close). And if that natural tendency is not monitored, it will find us at polar ends of the landscape.

My Greatest Ministry

I am realizing that my greatest ministry will be in the *next* generation. The life of David reminded me of that some weeks ago.

There came a point where he started storing gold and building materials so that his boy Solomon would have a free hand in building the Lord's temple. He had to switch his thinking when his life crossed the halfway point. He had to coach more and do less. His greatest contribution would be leading others to their greatest potential rather than accomplishing more personally. Of course he would still achieve much more, but he would soon come to grips with his humanity.

Now as a grandparent, I am finding that truth coming to bear on my life in ever-increasing ways. My responsibility doesn't end where my empty nest begins. It continues. (I offer a silent prayer here.) It must carry on into the generation of my grandchildren. I am not done yet!

Exodus 10:2 gives us our initial glimpse of this assignment. Here is the New Living Translation: "You will be able to tell wonderful stories to your *children and grandchildren* about the marvelous things I am doing among the Egyptians to prove that I am the Lord" (emphasis added).

Deuteronomy 4:9 tells us: "Do not forget the things which your eyes have seen and [be sure that] they do not depart from your heart all the days of your life; but make them known to your *sons and your grandsons*" (emphasis added).

At the time of this writing, I have two grandchildren and another on the way. I hope to have my quiver full of them one day, and I know that my influence cannot be apart from them. It must be inclusive of them, and that inclusion is intentional. No one else will fight for this. I must.

I have chosen to spend time with my family. I travel to Oregon and spend time with my children and *their children*. It's a biblical mandate. I have a small farm where I love sitting on a tractor and working with animals. It's therapeutic for me and it gives me contact with my children. We can live anywhere we choose to, but Anna and I have chosen to live where our family resides. It's not a decision based on geography, economics, landscape, or weather (although you can't beat Hawaii for weather). But since I have one son in Hawaii and two daughters in Oregon, I will do my best to spend a portion of my time in both of those places in the days ahead.

Now, some see me spending time in the Northwest and choose to paint it with dark colors. There will always be those who will try to make your decisions for you and judge your lifestyle as less than righteous. I will absorb all such criticism, and so must you.

Fight for your family.

If you don't, no one else will.

———

Reflections

What gave me the most hope during my season of wrestling with burnout was my wife. Also, my children and my support network kept reinforcing, "You will get better."

The night I experienced my meltdown I felt the Lord speak to me from Psalm 41:3: "The Lord will sustain him upon his sickbed; in his illness, You restore him to health." I declare that Scripture every night and have not missed a night since.

Today my marriage is better than ever. I realize what my wife did for me. She had to hold everything together. It strengthened our marriage.

Now I spend more time in my physical world: riding bikes, walking, and fishing. And the best moment for me is a quiet coffee with my best friend, my wife. Before, Sabbaths were optional extras. It isn't so anymore. That doesn't mean they are easy for me, but I have to take the time for my health and ministry.

I have made some major internal and external changes in the way I live and think. First, I had to change my old way of thinking. For years, it didn't matter how qualified I was. I have nine years of advanced theological training, but I still felt stupid.

144 - LEADING ON EMPTY

The second change I've made in my thinking is realizing that I can't do any more than I can do, and if people don't like it that's no fault of mine.

Third, nothing is that urgent.

—LEADER FROM AUSTRALIA

Chapter Nine:
Finding the Way Back Home

"Thus says the Lord:
'Stand in the ways and see,
And ask for the old paths, where the good way is,
And walk in it;
Then you will find rest for your souls.'"

JEREMIAH 6:16 NKJV

The sooner you wade out of the swampland of depression and back to solid ground again, the better.

I'm not saying to jump back into life at the pace you were unable to sustain previously, and I'm not saying to find some quick fix that shortcuts the process a loving God wants to walk you through. I'm simply saying get to the *resolution side* of the equation as quickly as possible—without unnecessary delay. A good amount of solitude and counsel are required to gain accurate assessment on the analysis side, but don't camp there. You won't tie up all the loose ends—not now, and maybe with some strands, not ever.

Loose ends are simply a part of life for everyone on this planet.

The journey out of depression and burnout may take a while, but remember this: Most of the changes will happen along the way back home. Waiting for the full download before you start on the road to healing will leave you with false hopes. Living in a de-motivated state is something that must be faced . . . and conquered. Waiting for depression to end before you begin to live will only compound the problem—and drain the batteries of your soul.

> "Most of the important things in the world have been accomplished by people who have kept on trying when there seemed to be no hope at all."
>
> **DALE CARNEGIE**

I remember going through knee surgery several years ago. No sooner had the procedure been completed than the nurse pulled me off the gurney and instructed me to walk.

Walk? Are you kidding me? All I really wanted to do was to take another pain pill and lie for a few more days under the warm blankets in post-op. But that didn't seem to be an acceptable option for this nurse.

She knew that the sooner I got my blood circulating, the sooner the healing would begin. Of course my movements would be restricted to ensure that I sustained no further damage, *but I had to start moving* whether I liked it or not.

PAINTING YOUR PREFERRED FUTURE

We are making an agreement in writing; and on the sealed document are the names of our leaders, our Levites and our priests. . . . The rest of the people . . . are joining with their kinsmen, their nobles . . . to keep and to observe all the commandments of

GOD our Lord, and His ordinances and His statutes. (Nehemiah 9:38; 10:28–29)

What I am about to share is an axiom for life. Don't miss this lesson.

In the wonderful book of Nehemiah, the people gathered together and made a covenant to which all the nobles, elders, and leaders affixed their signatures. This covenant would establish their trajectory toward a God-oriented preferred future. This was done at a time when they had spent nearly a whole day before the Lord in praise, worship, and listening to His Word.

Commitments to a preferred future do not come randomly. They are intentionally established at times when you are thinking clearly and are close to God.

Then with clarity of mind, they set these covenant standards on paper and committed themselves to carrying them out. It was written down because they knew that when their emotions changed about how they were to live and conduct themselves, they could refer back and navigate by these standards. Even when they could not see, they would pilot their decisions by these markings.

Commitments to a preferred future do not come randomly. They are intentionally established at times when you are thinking clearly and are close to God. They are not made impetuously, nor when you are in a slump, discouraged, depressed, or in a physical setback. Neither are these course markers established when you are overly optimistic or in some idealistic mood.

In the clearest of times, when you are near to Christ and thinking with insight rather than with ambiguity, imagine your ideal future. Write down that picture and how it can best be attained. *You must write it down.* Write down what your priority relationships will be that must remain healthy regardless of how you feel or what happens: your relationship with Christ and your relationship with your spouse and family.

Also answer these key questions:

- How do you want to be seen in ten years?
- What do you want to be good at or known for?
- What kind of personality do you want to have?
- What do you want your family to look like?

The more clearly you identify your target, the more apt you will be to hit it!

WRITE IT DOWN!

Habakkuk 2:2 instructs us in this manner: "Record the vision and inscribe it on tablets, that the one who reads it may run."

It is utterly important to write down your hope for a preferred future. Why? Because there will be times when pessimism may overtake optimism and discouragement may disqualify your joy, but this will not change the picture of your preferred future. What is not written down will become diluted into good intentions—shallow and replaceable by changing moods and impetuous moments. A life lived on this basis will be filled with insecurity, ambivalence, and indecision. Although those down times will inevitably come, you will know that the picture of your preferred future was written when you were *clear-headed, healthy, and close to Christ.*

But what if your life decisions *were* made in a negative state of mind? What would your life and disposition look like? If major decisions were spawned when you felt lonely and self-centered, when you felt no one supported you, wouldn't they be faulty at best? Your preferred future would be out of reach.

During my time of solitude, I asked God to silence every voice but His own. In those days, I wrote down the best picture I could of my preferred future: with regard to my faith, marriage, family, finances, ministry, physical health, and relationships. I prioritized them, reedited them, prayed over them, and revisited them after a week. (You will find a detailed list in chapter 5 under the subheading "The Most Important Five Percent.")

RUNNING IN HOPE

> For I know the plans that I have for you, declares the LORD, plans for welfare and not for calamity *to give you a future and a hope*. (Jeremiah 29:11, emphasis added)

Hope is a picture of a preferred future that does not diminish or tarnish with the changing moods of life. It is that vision you wrote down when you were clear-headed and close to Christ. It is what would delight God and be the optimum plan for your life and future.

That picture is still in the form of hope. But it will act as your GPS or your navigational beacon when emotions sag or energy flags. It corrects you back to what's most important and gives you hope, and it is hope that will give you sustainable energy.

Coming out of burnout, learn to *run with hope*.

SUSTAINING ENERGY

First Corinthians 13:13 tells us: "Now faith, hope, and love abide" (ESV).

We know about *faith* (our vertical relationship with God) and *love* (our

> "Many men owe the grandeur of their lives to their tremendous difficulties."
>
> **CHARLES H. SPURGEON**

horizontal relationships with others), but we don't hear much about *hope*.

Hope is the *sustaining energy* needed to accomplish the other two: to increase your relationship with Christ and to love those around you. Without hope, you will have the *knowledge* of the other two, but you will not have the *energy* to do anything about it. Without hope, you will *know* everything there is to know about faith, but your own faith will flag. You'll *know* everything there is to know about love, but the expression will not be genuine. It is hope—a picture of your preferred future—that will give you the sustenance needed to press through to your highest potential regardless of what your circumstances or surroundings look like.

Do you have a picture of your future? What does it look like? Have you written it down so that you may run?

"Never, never, never give up! And never give in except to convictions of honor and good sense."

WINSTON CHURCHILL

During the days of your rehabilitation, at times you will need to start running when the feelings have not yet arrived. You may have restructured and re-calibrated your navigational beacons, but your desire will be flagging.

You will run in the *hope* of finishing well.

There is great hope for every person who has experienced what it means to lead on empty. There will be wisdom and energy that comes no other way: to finish strong, without accepting a lowered ceiling, you must learn to live by hope.

The writer of Hebrews weighs in with a similar piece of encouragement: "This hope we have as an anchor of the soul, both sure and steadfast" (Hebrews 6:19 NKJV).

Hope is an anchor for our souls. A mother will set her alarm clock for a certain time. She hopes in the clock's dependability; she sleeps soundly knowing the alarm will sound on schedule.

We fly on airplanes when we have no real grasp of the laws of aerodynamics, yet we rest in the hope that the pilots are well trained and competent and the planes have been serviced, tested, and well maintained.

> The LORD is faithful to all his promises and loving toward all he has made. (Psalm 145:13 NIV)

At some point in my healing process, I had to anchor my soul on hope—hope that I would return to wholeness, that my marriage would be wonderful, and that my family would be healthy—even though I couldn't see it happening at the time. I knew I had to live by hope. There were days when I simply kept motoring forward, even though I had to tow my feelings behind me. I pressed on in the knowledge that God would be faithful.

Imagine a person running to catch a bus. He knows that the bus arrives at that stop every morning at exactly 8:30. It has been there for the past five years without fail. So being a bit tardy leaving his house, he runs toward the bus stop *knowing* that the bus will arrive at the scheduled time. The bus is still nowhere in sight. It hasn't rounded the corner onto his street. Passers-by may even make comments as to the futility of his actions when there is no visible proof, but he runs *in the hope* that the bus driver will be faithful to his schedule.

> "The greater the obstacle, the more glory in overcoming it."
>
> **MOLIERE**

We serve a God who never fails us when we run in the confidence of His trustworthiness. He gives us a "hope [that] does not disappoint" (Romans 5:5). When we run with His promises in mind, we will not be weary.

Paul the apostle reminds us that "the plowman ought to plow in hope, and the thresher to thresh in hope of sharing the crops" (1 Corinthians 9:10).

FINDING A LIFE COACH

There may be times when finding that picture of a preferred future requires some assistance. You may need help as you heal and re-calibrate. In the beginning, your times of solitude will serve you well, but as you move past the critical red zone of burnout and depression, finding a life coach may increase your chances of successful reentry. While it is not mandatory, it can prove helpful. It's akin to retaining the services of a trainer when you're trying to lose weight and strengthen your muscles. These certified consultants will check your pace and stride. They will put you through some personality profiles, temperament tests, and help you develop a life plan.

During this time, I spent some hours with a ministry friend, Craig Chong, who took me through the Birkman Profile. It was developed by Dr. Roger Birkman, in 1951, as a result of research conducted at the University of Texas. Craig paced me through my tendencies and personality quirks, affirming what drained me and what filled me. We talked about legacy and fruitfulness, focus and passion.

I also met with an old friend of mine. Business consultant and strategist Tom Paterson authored the book *Living the Life You Were Meant to Live*. He helped me navigate my life as I came out of the woods of burnout and to understand how to convert suffering into something beneficial.

I spent a day with him at his home in Grants Pass, Oregon. He is a man who has suffered much, and through it he has fully surrendered to the will of Christ. First, his twelve-year-old daughter, Debbie, died of cancer. Then his wife, Ginny, after fifty years of marriage, went to heaven. Shortly thereafter, his son Tom was killed in an airplane accident, and then he lost another son to an automobile accident. My friend Tom remarried, but his wife passed away five months later.

In his humble home, I sat with a towering respect for this eighty-one-year-old saint who understood suffering more than most. I asked him, "Tom, you have suffered more than ten men. What has kept you from bitterness?"

He paused and said, "After my daughter, Debbie, died at twelve years old, I had a ring made for my wife—a band fashioned out of three strands. One was for her, the other was for me, and the third was for Jesus, who held us all together. That is what I have learned."

He slowly continued: "Wayne, we must come to a point where we fully surrender to Christ. Nothing held back. And the events of great suffering in your life will bring you to that point. You can choose to recede or you can choose to surrender. I chose to surrender."

FIND A TITUS

> But God, who comforts the depressed, *comforted us by the coming of Titus.* (2 Corinthians 7:6, emphasis added)

While finding a professional life coach may not be a mandate for rehabilitation, finding a wise Christian friend who knows how to listen certainly is. A friend can help you navigate this new season and calibrate your compass accurately. He can help you find the hope of your preferred future—not another pipe dream, but a vision God has given to you as your calling and purpose.

> God gave burdens, also shoulders.
>
> **YIDDISH SAYING**

Arriving at the right life plan, that *accurate hope* of a preferred future, may require a Titus—someone who will offer an objective viewpoint of you, your life, your gifts, and your passions. It is God who ultimately comforts the depressed, but sometimes He uses people to deliver His comfort.

Find a Titus for yourself. This may be a professional counselor, a support group, or someone who is older than you (or at least older in the faith). It could be an elder in your church, a pastor, or a businessperson. Take the initiative to approach a potential Titus and say, "Can we have coffee together sometime? I need to talk about something I'm going through."

I've been honored to have several Tituses in my life. These are people who love Jesus and who love me—in that order. They're around if you'll keep your eyes open for them.

In this season of life, don't make the mistake of thinking you are self-sufficient. God made you a *part* of His body, and each part needs the others to survive.

Friends are rare these days, but it is not because they have diminished in importance. It is because we have increased in speed. Friendships are not made in the blur of life. They are made in the margins. Margins, like the white space around the words on this page that you are reading, add to the composition and overall fabric of the whole. Without margins, the words would crowd one another and fight for space, making it unreadable. Of course, if the printer extended the words from one end of the page to the other without a break, it would reduce the book by fifty pages or so, save trees, and cost less. But who would read it? It would be a futile exercise in stress management! No book ever begrudges its margins.

And no life should either.

One of the benefits of margins is that this is where friends are found. Friends are God's gifts to us. An anonymous saying reminds us of their value: "A friend is one to whom you can pour out the contents of your heart, chaff and grain alike, knowing that the gentlest of hands will take and sift it, keep what is worth keeping, and with a breath of kindness, blow the rest away."

In 1 Kings 4:4–5, Solomon actually made official the office of a friend. As he appointed his cabinet, he added one more office: "Benaiah the son of Jehoiada was over the army; and Zadok and

Abiathar were priests; and Azariah the son of Nathan was over the deputies; and Zabud the son of Nathan, a priest, was *the king's friend"* (emphasis added).

Dan Shima was my dear friend and partner in ministry. He has since retired, but during our years together, he was a spiritual director to me. We met regularly to discuss my spiritual life. Knowing my temperament and personality, he could tailor his encouragement and directives to where I was in my journey at that time.

Suffering will change you, but not necessarily for the better. You have to choose that!

You must remember that a pastor's spiritual life is somewhat different from that of the members of a congregation. Don't discount the value of having someone else monitor your spiritual journey. A Russian proverb says, "The eye cannot see the eye." When you take time to meet with a spiritual mentor, he can help keep you spiritually alive and fit for the rest of your journey. Doing this will help you not only restore but also increase your hunger for what God has called you to do.

LEANING ON OTHERS

Charlie Wedemeyer is a dear friend of our church. He was born in Honolulu and was a football standout at Punahou, a prestigious private high school. He then played football for Michigan State, and while coaching football at Los Gatos High School, he was diagnosed with Lou Gehrig's disease. It took such a toll on his body that today he is able to move only his lips and eyebrows. He and his wife, Lucy, travel extensively, giving people hope in a broken world. Each time he has been with us, we leave the auditorium thinking, *What problems do I have? Absolutely none!*

Charlie has to have someone else do everything for him: feed him, clothe him, bathe him, shave him, and even help him to the bathroom. Even his breathing apparatus, if not maintained by another person, will cause him to suffocate.

All the while being completely and utterly dependent on others, God has used him in mighty ways to touch the lives of millions—bringing inspiration and new motivation to many.

When we wrestle with our own infirmities, we are not disqualified from God's plan for our lives. It may just mean we will arrive at it differently from the way we had intended. We may arrive leaning on the arm of a friend.

> ## The very nature of the healing process will require that you disclose your feelings and inward pain. *Just make sure that your sympathetic friend doesn't become a fatal attraction.*

Which brings me to an important warning: The very nature of the healing process will require that you disclose your feelings and inward pain. Bruised emotions and depression can yearn for safe harbors and hiding places. *Just make sure that your sympathetic friend doesn't become a fatal attraction.* Heed this simple mandate: *Guys with the guys and girls with the girls.*

DIVINE MENTORS

Regardless of whether you use a life coach or try to navigate on your own, there is one indispensable principle you cannot compromise: You need divine mentors.

Every mistake, every pitfall, and every poor decision you could ever make has already been made and recorded somewhere in the pages of the Old and New Testaments. It may not match your situation detail for detail, but the principles will be right on target, and the solutions you need will be right at hand.

Every mistake, every pitfall, and every poor decision you could ever make has already been made and recorded somewhere in the Bible.

> All Scripture is inspired by God and is useful for teaching the truth, rebuking error, correcting faults, and giving instruction for right living, so that the person who serves God may be fully qualified and equipped. (2 Timothy 3:16–17 TEV)

Let me reiterate a deeper source of guidance than human counsel. Remember: Everything you have gone through, someone in the Bible has gone through before you.

Elijah struggled with depression. Joseph struggled with abandonment. David met with discouragement and distress. Let these mentors walk through those seasons with you.

This part of your rehabilitation is nonnegotiable. Friends and life coaches may come and go, but there is one Friend and Life Coach who will walk with you through all the days of your life—right on into eternity. To hear His voice every day, be sure to develop the discipline of daily devotions.

A very simple way to begin is to start with the book of Proverbs. This book has thirty-one chapters, and like taking a one-a-day multivitamin, you read a chapter a day. Match the day to the chapter, so if it is the tenth of the month, simply read Proverbs 10. Choose one verse that the Holy Spirit seems to highlight just for you. Then using the acrostic SOAP, write a

> "Good timber does not grow with ease; the stronger the wind, the stronger the trees."
>
> **J. WILLARD MARRIOTT**

reflection of that in a notebook. *S* stands for the Scripture. Write it down. *O* is for an observation—write down what it is saying to you. It can be just a few sentences. *A* asks you to make an application to your life. How will you be different today because of what you have just read? Don't leave the Bible without an application. Choose to be renewed by what you have read. Then finally, *P* stands for prayer—write down something that you are asking God to help you with. Your journaling will assist you in gaining insight from your experiences, and it will help you navigate the days ahead.

Emotional and spiritual health won't happen in a day, but they will *improve daily*. You can't compromise this part of your life. None of us can! Daily time with God in the pages of His Word and in prayer is foundational, and no building, however architecturally beautiful it might be, will stand without a deep foundation.

The story is told of a farmer who owned an orchard in a valley full of orchards. One year the drought was harsher than all the previous years. Yet his trees were verdant and more fruitful than the surrounding ones. The other farmers' trees were brown while his were still green. They gathered one day to ask his secret.

He replied, "My trees can go another four weeks without water. You see, when they were young, I often withheld water from them so that their roots were forced to drill deeper to find water. So while other trees are dying, mine are drinking from a much deeper source." Drill down, and get your water from a deeper source.

GET 'ER DONE!

My season of burnout convinced me that I needed to restructure my life. That would be the most difficult part of my task. I was good at *locating* the problems. A leadership sense combined with thirty-four years of pastoring taught me how to do that well. I had a keen eye for what others needed to do in order to correct *their lives*.

But now it was my turn.

The secret to success has always been a bias for action. Without it, nothing changes. The old cowboys used to say, "Just get 'er done!"

How would I live differently? What course corrections would I make? There could be no repeats. Who knows if I could even survive a second wave of emotional depletion? So I had to get serious about the route I would take.

FOUR LIFE COURSES . . . CHOOSE ONE

There are four basic courses by which we can live. These may not be planned, but they will be followed regardless. Every life follows a set of rules, a default of ideals that may have been caught more than taught. I had to look at each one individually and intentionally choose my route. So will you. This one choice will alter your future once and for all, and opting out will default you to one of the first three.

1. A Life of Reaction

With this paradigm—a life of reaction—we plod forward until something forces us to change direction. The loss of a job will compel us to find another. The perceived acceptance of one or the rejection of another will dictate our circle of friendships. The initiative of another person toward us determines our course, but without it, we aren't motivated to action.

A life of reaction is a life lived in the twilight realms between conservatism and activism, hope and dejection, passive indifference and compulsive hyperactivity. It is a disorienting, sometimes dangerous way to live, but the majority of people have chosen this lifestyle, most of them by default.

2. A Life of Conformity

With this mindset—a life of conformity—we live according to the view of the crowd. We float along on the current of popular opinion. We tend to gravitate to trends for our sense of well-being. We allow how we look to trump what we believe, and we permit what others think to drive what we do. This course of life usually enrolls those who feel best when they are needed and who thrive on being liked. These people wrestle with appearances and grapple with perceptions. It is another dangerous way to live. It puts you at the mercy of opinion.

> "There is no failure except in no longer trying."
>
> **ELBERT HUBBARD**

Author and professor Leo Buscaglia once said, "The easiest thing to be in the world is you. The most difficult thing to be is what other people want you to be. Don't let them put you in that position."

3. A Life of Independence

Men and women who choose a life of independence cherish the illusion of autonomy. But when they group together with other like-minded people, carefully steering away from the current majority, they form a clan of virtual clones. Maybe it's buying organic this-or-that, spurning anything genetically modified. Or perhaps it's showing disdain for the "old school" by sporting a body covered with tattoos. Whatever sets them apart and unto themselves is trendy so long as it distinguishes them from the herd of the former generation. It can be a self-delusional way to live.

4. A Life of Intentionality

A life of intentionality is the restructured life I chose, and I am writing this book to encourage you to do the same.

When we were young, life happened as a matter of course. When we were hungry, food appeared, fully prepared by a parent or sibling. School was just out there—ready for us to plug in and participate. Making friends was basically a slam dunk; all we needed was another recess, and we returned with an armload of new chums. And for the most part, our weight remained stable. We could eat whatever we wanted and yet stay fit and slim.

No more!

Somewhere along the line, things moved from automatic to manual, from natural to deliberate, and from involuntary to intentional. You are not told when the switch takes place, but if you don't make that transition, you will always be behind the eight ball. It happens at different times for different people, but it does take place! The evolution comes without warning and it happens without your permission.

Your marriage, which early on seemed to maintain itself, will no longer survive the way it used to. Healthy marriages require intentionality and planned investment. So will your waistline, your family, your ministry, your faith, and your emotional health. The Scriptures exhort us to "run in such a way that you may win" (1 Corinthians 9:24). It is not automatic.

> "There is no doubt that it is around the family and the home that all the greatest virtues, the most dominating virtues of human society, are created, strengthened, and maintained."
>
> **WINSTON CHURCHILL**

If you *choose to win*, you have achieved half the victory. If you do not choose, you have gained half your defeat.

SOME THINGS YOU NEVER GIVE UP ON

My youngest daughter is one of the treasures in my life. We adopted her three days after birth, and since that day, she's been the apple of my eye. However, several years ago, she made some choices that compromised her faith and morality. She was expelled from college and later moved across the country from her family. Her actions caused great distress to my wife and me. As an adopted child, she wrestled with her conflicted identity and her birth parents' choice to give her up for adoption.

My first response was just to let her be because of her choice to disenfranchise herself from her family. But I also knew this wasn't a choice I had the privilege of making. My choice to keep my family close was not dependent on my children's acceptance of that value. It was something that I had intentionally decided to keep as part of my "What's Most Important" list. This is something that is decided beforehand—so that it will survive an attack. Once that happens, once a cataclysmic event takes place, it's too late to make that decision. You can only navigate by buoys already set in place.

So my wife and I continued to contact her by phone, letter, and e-mail. Giving up was not an option, regardless of her choices. Anna would send Abby truths gleaned from her devotions and cover her with prayer. Often my wife's attempts would go unheeded and my phone messages unanswered. Nevertheless, for two years we continued to pray and write and call.

My goal in life is not necessarily to get rich, but to BE RICH!

One day Anna received an e-mail from our daughter that included something gleaned from *her devotions*. I was pleasantly surprised to find out that she had once again returned to His presence. Her devotional insights included these words:

> "I know now that God may not have had me born *of* this family, but I am convinced that He has had me born *into* this family. I am coming home!"

Don't you think we became rich that day?

You see, my goal in life is not necessarily to get rich. It is to BE RICH—in my faith, my marriage, my family, and my ministry. It is a choice that I made when I defined what *rich* would mean. It is an attitude, a value, a decision, *an intention.*

Choose to live life on purpose, to love intentionally, and to plan accordingly!

———

Reflections

Dear Pastor Wayne:

Thank you for staying in the fight. Over the past year I realized that the time in my life that God used you to finally get through to me, you were fighting a battle of your own. But you didn't quit. I don't fully understand what all of your struggles were, but this I do know: At your lowest point in ministry, Jesus found me because you didn't give up.

You taught me how to journal. You taught me how to begin each day intimately with Jesus. You taught me the significance of having a divine mentor in my life each day. In forty years, you were the first to show me how to listen to Jesus through His precious Word. And I have begun to change. The Lord has opened my eyes to many things I wish I had learned long ago. The Spirit of God exudes from you and it is obvious that you meet with Him every day.

Thank you so much for staying the course and being a friend and mentor to me.

—A SERVICEMAN AND MEMBER OF OUR CONGREGATION

Chapter Ten
The Intentional Life

"For this reason we must pay much closer attention to what we have heard, so that we do not drift away from it."

HEBREWS 2:1

Living an intentional life includes consistent monitoring and assessment. Entropy, or the gradual decline back into a mediocre lifestyle defined by habit and reaction, is natural. This chapter will suggest how to restructure your days in order to live an intentional life.

Sadly, what we do not observe willingly is often imposed upon us forcefully. Sickness, ministry fatigue, an emotional breakdown, a moral failure, or giving up will cause a compulsory stoppage or reduction in ministry. But often it seems more permissible if the time off is due to a breakdown rather than to the wisdom of avoiding it. I experienced that. You won't need to.

A healthy life cadence contributes a great deal to being a healthy pastor or Christian leader. It is that daily, weekly, and monthly regimen that can point you toward a life of abundance without regrets. It may not produce celebrity status, nor does it guarantee that you will appear on the latest *Forbes* list. But it can help prepare you to stand before God, as Paul describes in Colossians 1:22: "holy and blameless and beyond reproach."

We will all experience fatigue in the midst of a demanding ministry unless time is set aside to rest and realign ourselves back to God and His original design.

MUSCLE CARS

I used to be like a muscle car without full traction, complete with spinning tires and flying gravel. I would fishtail from side to side, burning rubber in great clouds, and with some spectacle, I would make forward progress.

But I am finding that I can move forward at the same pace if I slow down in order to gain full traction—and use that traction to proceed without fishtailing, effectively saving energy and minimizing wasted motion. I don't make as much of a spectacle as I used to, but I think I can do without that.

"Balance is enjoying life, enjoying work, spending time with family and friends, keeping healthy, playing, maintaining spirituality, and giving back to the community."

WWW.ENERPACE.COM/
BALANCED_LIFE_
ARTICLE.PDF

TOOLS FOR LIFE

There are several tools that have helped me to live a more intentional life after I returned from my journey. One is the *Life Calendar*. This monthly calendar helps me to live intentionally. I developed it after I realized the importance of the intentional life. Each month gives you tools to plan, stay on track, check your progress, and stay true to your devotions, family, and health. You may order this from *www.lifejournal.cc*.

The *Life Calendar* helps me live an intentional life.

With this tool, I gauge the speed and accuracy with which I am living my life. It has daily, weekly, and seasonal components that I must assess and maintain. It may not include an exhaustive list of what I do, but it helps me to monitor what is most important. When those nonnegotiables are lined up, the rest seem to fall into place much more easily.

Here is a rhythm, or a *life cadence*, I try to maintain:

LIFE CADENCE:

Daily—Basics

- I limit the number of evenings I am not at home with my family (spouse) to no more than three in a row (and so should you). Here are a few guidelines:
  - One evening of ministry—of course
  - Two evenings in a row—okay
  - Three evenings in a row—possible, but I first ask my wife and family for their specific permission

• Four evenings in a row—No! There's got to be a better way.

- Remember to reserve a pocket of energy for home and for yourself!

- To ensure that I fulfill the daily necessities of life, I use the acrostic **PEPRD** to keep the spice of life alive.

  • P = Prayer—Always spend at least a few minutes in prayer to connect your soul with God's heart.

  • E = Exercise—Do some amount of exercise every day, even if it is a regimen of core exercises in the privacy of your own living room.

  • P = Planning—Take time to plan your day, your month, and prepare your heart for the people and tasks you are about to encounter.

  • R = Reading—Read something every day. It could be a magazine or a book of choice in order to increase your knowledge, give you fresh ideas, and renew your interest in life.

  • D = Devotions—Never allow the day to swallow up your personal time with God.

Weekly—Six days of labor /a "Sabbath" day

- Obey God's Word and take a day off! It honors Him when we do. If you are a pastor, try for a day early in the week when your mind is uncluttered by the looming weekend service.

- It might help to read either of these books by Richard Swenson (NavPress) when planning your week:

  • *The Overload Syndrome: Learning to Live Within Your Limits*

  • *Margin: Restoring Emotional, Physical, Financial, and Time Reserves to Overloaded Lives*

- Plan your Sabbath day with activities that fill your tank: golf, fishing, exercise, puttering around the house, gardening, whatever works for you. Change the pace! Get personal things done that you've wanted to do for a long time, but make sure it is relaxing and/or fun. You need a recharge day.

- Take extra time having your devotions that day. Savor your time with God and do some extra studies to dig deeper. Fill your soul to the brim.

Seasonal—Personal Retreat Days and Holidays

- Establish a monthly *Personal Retreat Day* (PRD) away from your office and centered on God's agenda. I will explain this further in the following pages.

- Get into the habit of making holidays fun events for your family.

- Think of the depth of the relationship Job had with his sons and daughters (and their families) by having them over to the house for a meal and taking time to pray for each one. Have the whole family over and bring in extra chairs!

- Make everybody's birthday in your immediate family a special day.

- Celebrate often. It renews relationships and makes your faith something easy to live with and attractive. Never think of celebrating as unspiritual.

- Think of the memories generated as families celebrated the Feast of Tabernacles by building tents and living in them for a week. Try camping!

Family powwows are to discuss our futures, plans, and dreams. If there are any relational snafus, we take time to resolve them.

- Family Powwows—I take time seasonally to bring all my children around a table, and we discuss our futures, plans, and dreams. If there are any relational snafus, we take time to resolve them and rectify whatever miscommunication there may be. I mediate these and ensure that there is nothing left unresolved or any remaining unforgiveness. These have proven to be one of the best things we have done as a family. We started these gatherings after I returned from my burnout. I wish we had started them sooner! All the family must be present for these. No exceptions. In the past year we have had two family meetings.

Seasons of Life—Restorative Sabbaticals

- After seven years of consistent ministry, take a three-month sabbatical to renew your hunger.

- Get away for a time of healing and, if possible, go somewhere that will energize you with new ideas and resources in the middle of your sabbatical.

- Your mind will begin to be hungry again, and you will pick up ideas that you can take home. If you do this in the middle of your sabbatical, it will still give you a few weeks to process through the ideas and get your creative juices flowing again.

- Read books, such as Bob Buford's *Half Time*, that will help steer you away from a midlife crisis and into a midlife renewal.

Don't wait to begin practicing this life cadence until after you crash. Start by honoring the daily, weekly, and seasonal calls to rest. No one but you needs to give you permission to do that.

Your personal retreat day gives you a chance to get the scattered pieces of your life back in order and bring clarity and focus back to your life. It gives you a prolonged opportunity to talk with God and let Him talk to you.

PERSONAL RETREAT DAY

A monthly personal retreat day has proven to be extremely helpful to me. I am grateful to the Evangelical Free Church of America for this idea. Their Recovery Church Ministry has helped hundreds of pastors and leaders. You can get more help from their excellent Web site: *www.efca.org.*

PRD Schedule

Your personal retreat day is a monthly day out of the office. Schedule it into your calendar. There's nothing mystical about it. It simply gives you a chance to get the scattered pieces of your life back in order. It helps to clear the fog and bring clarity and focus back to your life. This is crucial to living an intentional life. Most important, it gives you a prolonged opportunity to talk with God and let Him talk to you.

It's not necessarily a time when you sit quietly and wait for revelations from God. That kind of plan will find you asleep within the hour. Instead, bring along some inspirational music, your calendar/planner, a notebook, a pen, your Bible, a laptop computer if you have one (but not for e-mail). Don't come with a full agenda. It's a time to plan, think, reflect, and look forward. Here is what I currently do on my personal retreat day:

Part One—First, I do a short run to get my blood moving! Then I take an extended time for my devotions. I start at 6:30 AM, and I pore over the Scriptures, being careful to enjoy my time of writing in my journal. I don't rush it. I then take time to pray, write down a list of ways I need to apply what God has been teaching me, and how I will live differently because of what He has said. I ask God to silence every voice but His own. I usually spend two hours on this section.

Part Two—Next, I take out my calendar and review where I have been. I check myself to see if I have been faithful to my top 5 percent of responsibilities that God has asked of me: my faith, marriage, family, ministry, and health; then I check to see if I am enjoying life. I review what needs attention and what areas of my life need more emphasis. I note these in my *Life Calendar*. I plan my times of rest, breaks, and family gatherings. These I schedule in advance, because life has a tendency to crowd out what's most important. I always set those foundation stones in first. This takes me about one hour.

Part Three—I spend about two hours on this section. I look at my speaking schedule and upcoming sermons. I plan them out in advance so I can increase the preparation time. I take time to hear what God is saying to our church, and I write this out in themes. I explain this more fully in our leadership practicums held three times a year. I am usually able to accomplish the first three parts of my personal retreat day in the morning.

Part Four—I grade the dials on my *dashboard*. I explain this in the upcoming section, "My Twelve Dials." I get brutally honest with how I am doing in certain critical areas of my life that are not readily visible. Then I prioritize anything that sags beneath a B- average, writing down how I will improve the grade by my next personal retreat day. This takes me an hour at the most.

Schedule a day to get alone with God, to renew your soul, and restore your hunger for what He has called you to do.

Part Five—I then do some message preparation and reading. Some of the books that have been beneficial to me have been missionary biographies. The lives of wonderful people such as Hudson Taylor, Jonathan Goforth, David Livingston, Mother Teresa, and Amy Carmichael have always proved to stir my soul. I do this for about two hours.

Part Six—I take the final part of my day to dream. I write down what I need to do in the next five years: goals that I want to accomplish; an environment I want for my family; ideas for our marriage; trips I have always wanted to take; and other dreams.

Then I go home around six o'clock and have a wonderful dinner with my wife, letting her in on all the dreams I had! She always has a special way of helping me sift through and separate the lesser dreams from the ones that sparkle.

My personal retreat day format may not necessarily work for you, but it can give you a start. The point is to schedule a day to get alone with God, to renew your soul, and restore your hunger for what He has called you to do. It will help you to clarify your future, refocus your heart, and reenlist! It is a holy day—one that will help to make you more effective in life and ministry.

Tips for a Successful Personal Retreat Day

1. If you don't schedule it, it won't happen. And if you are a pastor, try to plan it toward the end of the month on a Monday or Tuesday. Having it at the end of the month enables you to assess how you did and plan for the upcoming month.

2. A personal retreat day is not a catch-up day. Leave the e-mails and unfinished tasks on your desk. Delegate them or leave them till you get back, but do not fill your personal retreat day with uncompleted items. If you come back refreshed and renewed, you will have more energy and insight to finish what has been patiently awaiting your return.

3. Don't hold your personal retreat day at your church. I would even suggest not having it at your home (unless you have a second home, away from home). I find a place with few distractions. I have tried various locations. I have gone to another pastor's church where they've made an empty office available. I sometimes go to a hotel and spend the money to *purchase* peace and quiet. I put a "Do Not Disturb"

sign on my door and put my headset on to minimize the extraneous noise. And if that is not possible, I find a library. Our university has a big one where I can find a quiet corner, and I bring my headset.

4. Plan it along the way. I am always jotting down notes and ideas I want to think through on my personal retreat day. I also write down Scriptures that have stirred me and that I want to study further. I may also pack a book or two that I want to peruse or a list of past goals I want to revisit. I take along something fun to read as well, such as a motorcycle or farming magazine or a trade journal of something I am interested in.

FINDING YOUR AIRPORT

As I mentioned earlier, another tool I have learned to use in living an intentional life besides the *Life Calendar* and the personal retreat day has been a *dashboard* of sorts so I can see what is not seen. These areas of life need to be healthy and vibrant, and when they sag, you will need to do whatever is necessary to recoup.

Let me explain.

I met a dear pastor friend of mine at a local airport as he was leaving town. He told me he had resigned from his pastorate a month prior. His family had been feeling the suffering taking place in his soul, and he felt he needed to renew his energy for life; he needed a new start.

I understood his sentiments. I encouraged and applauded him for staying true to his basic calling to be a man of God and a father to his family, even though his ministry would take on a new dimension. Whether he would one day return to the local church, he couldn't say. But he needed to renew his hunger.

My friend at the airport had been compelled to make some critical in-flight decisions. *He was about to land at a different airport than the one he'd set out for.* But this new airport was not a secondary one. Though it may not have been in his plans, it would turn out to be the airport God had in mind when He filed His flight plans before my friend was even born.

He was not abandoning his original calling. In fact, he was recovering it. After a needed sabbatical, he would find it, but in a different part of the vineyard. Today, he is exhilarated to be part of a missions outreach ministry, and you will find him sharing what God is doing in his life through miracles great and small.

MY TWELVE DIALS

Maybe it was because we were at an airport, but I couldn't help but think about an airline pilot watching his instruments. Sometimes those digital numbers will rise and sometimes they will fall. Some of the needles on the dials will go up, and some will go down. But if you happen to be responsible for an aircraft and its passengers, you will do well to pay close attention to those instruments. Ignoring them would be insane. In some emergency situations, the pilot will find it necessary to change flight plans and land at a secondary airport. Yes, a central concern is certainly getting from Point A to Point B in a timely fashion, but the lives and safety of those on board are more important.

A pilot understands this more than anyone else.

My "dashboard" includes twelve dials that meter vital systems essential to my health and success.

He is not able to see certain critical components that need to be monitored. He can't see the oil level. Neither can he readily observe the engine overheating. The gas level in the tank is out of his sight, and he cannot tell if the carburetor is icing. So he has meters and dials that are connected to these critical pieces of equipment, and they are placed on a dashboard directly in front of him. In this way, he is able to see and monitor these hidden parts. If one of them breaks, it's already too late. By monitoring his instruments, he can catch a problem in its early stages and, if necessary, land at a secondary airstrip.

There are several crucial areas of my life that are out of my sightline. They are not easily observable, but regardless, if they go faulty, not seeing them will not make everything okay. I'll still crash.

A tool that helps me see the unseen is my "dashboard." It includes twelve dials that meter vital systems essential to my health and success. I first delineate what they are; then I assess them. I am brutally honest in grading each of them. I then write a few sentences that give me direction in how to make improvements. I assign a letter grade to each area, and then I decide which ones require immediate maintenance and repair.

Your twelve dials will differ from mine, but find out what they are and monitor them before your aircraft begins to lose altitude.

I did this exercise on my personal retreat day a few weeks ago. Allow me to let you in on the results and the steps of action I will take for each:

1. Faith Life   B+

My faith life needs more consistency and cataloging of my thoughts and plans. I need to increase my devotional, theological, and skill-development reading.

2. Marriage Life   A-

My marriage life is going from good to great. I need to take more time with Anna so we can do things together: exercise, walks, talks, and other moments. I get too one-dimensional when ministry is at hand, so I need to see if I can cut out of ministry duties more often.

3. Family Life   A-

My family life is good. I love my kids and grandkids, am loyal and committed to their bright futures. I need to be closer to them for discipleship purposes and to be sure they are growing deeply in the things of God. I have plans for our future and how I can disciple them better while still being sensitive that I do not overly encroach on my children's personal lives.

4. Office Life   C-

My office life needs organizing. My files, home insurance, tax records, pending receipts, and other important papers are hard to find. I will purchase the book *One Thing at a Time: 100 Simple Ways to Live Clutter-Free Every Day* by Cindy Glovinsky and learn that everything has its place. I will set up my office to reflect excellence and ease of access. Neatness will help me to have a clearer head and feel more at peace. This will be done within the month.

5. Computer Life   C

Since I am on my computer a great deal, this has become a major part of my life. My computer serves as a cataloging system as well as a delivery system for what I do. I need to get larger hard drives to archive photos, smaller drives that are transportable to store videos (which I need to identify and collect) that I will use for traveling and speaking, and better use my Mac.com account for uploading the files I need as I am on the road. I will also de-clutter my computer's hard drive for optimum performance.

6. Ministry Life   B-

My ministry life is too crowded. I feel behind when it comes to training staff. I am working on a restructuring plan now and will reevaluate in four months. I will train and release a group of bi-vocational leaders to lead community campuses, and I will concentrate on training more future leaders.

7. Financial Life   B+

My financial picture is good, but my files and records could use some organizing. I have to take time (maybe a whole day) to assess my status. I will line it up with my plans for the future. My goal in life is not to get rich, but to *be rich*—in ministry, faith, family, marriage, and peace.

8. Social Life   B-

As I said, I can be too one-dimensional. I need to take time for a social life, develop friendships, and get involved in social activities. I used to do that better, but when the church began to grow, I zeroed in on ministry. I need to rebalance.

9. Attitudinal Life   B

I tend to get too discouraged with those I think should know better. I must be more patient or simply get away from those who deplete me. I will work on my patience and not impose my speed on others who cannot run as fast. But at the same time, I cannot let their speed become mine. I also need to improve my people skills. As a leader, I have the responsibility to train and to encourage, to correct and to discipline. The first ones are easy and the latter tasks are tough.

10. Author's Life   C

I am behind in my writing. I will make time for what God has given to me as a writing assignment. I will work on my next book.

11. Speaker's Life   B

As a speaker, I am to teach the body of Christ at large. I struggle with the balance of my calling—the time I must spend in our local church and the time I must spend elsewhere. I will take a season to deliberate before the Lord in order to catch His heart and balance in the matter.

12. Physical Life   B-

I want to lose more weight to reach and maintain my ideal weight. I know that I must take more time for that and prioritize it. I will also eat healthy and be moderate in all things.

THE AXIOM OF TRUTH

In each of these assessments, truth is irreducible. Truth is the foremost axiom of personal development. We will learn important lessons no matter how we choose to live, but we will accelerate our growth by deliberately turning away from falsehood and denial. Genuine growth is only found in honest growth. Our very first commitment must be to truth—the truth about ourselves, our failings, our shortcomings, our habits.

Genuine growth is only found in honest growth.

You cannot take shortcuts by going through the land of make-believe. Your first commitment must be to discover and accept new truths no matter how difficult or how unpleasant they may seem at the time. You cannot rectify problems if you deny that they exist. How will you achieve a fulfilled life if you won't admit that your current position is wrong for you? How can you improve your marriage if you refuse to admit that you feel empty on the inside? How can you improve your health if you won't admit that the habits you have are not serving God's purposes in your life?

The arbiter of truth will always be reality. Realizing truth will not necessarily guarantee success, but siding with falsehood is surely enough to guarantee failure!

When you side with truth, your problems may not disappear overnight, but you will have just taken a God-sized step in the right direction.

———

Reflections

A series of phone calls recently changed our lives. First, we found that my wife's father had just died. Then my grandson died on the operating table. He was just fifty-six days old, and during surgery the doctors closed the valve of his heart instead of opening it. In the middle of this my youngest daughter got pregnant outside of marriage. I have walked through grieving with others, but it is another thing to walk through it yourself. I buried my grandson and then went back to work the next day. The slide began to increase and I found myself despondent and unable to recoup my energy.

Last year I was at the convention in Washington, D.C. Inside the packet given to all the pastors was a one-page testimony from Pastor Wayne Cordeiro talking about his experience with burnout, causing him to take a sabbatical. I started to cry as I read that in the hotel room. My wife asked me what was wrong; I just handed her the paper and told her this was how I felt.

I went from Washington to New York State, where I was speaking at a church. I couldn't stop crying. When I returned home, I still couldn't stop. It was then that my staff told me that I needed to stop. So I just walked out of the office for a three-month sabbatical.

I contacted Focus on the Family, and they referred me to SonScape, a restoration camp for pastors and Christian leaders in Colorado (www.sonscape.org). It was the best eight days of my life.

I remember one story they told that helped particularly. They explained how a fish can handle the current. But if the fish remains indefinitely in that current, it cannot survive. Instead, the fish must choose to hide behind a rock, go deep beneath the current, or find a quiet pool. No one could guarantee that the pressures of ministry would diminish when we returned, but we as pastors could make the choice to hide, go deep, or find a quiet place.

I gave myself permission to grieve—not just the deaths, but all kinds of losses in my life. I had never given myself permission to grieve.

Did I come back perfect? No. This year has been a hard year for me. We lost some people when I went on sabbatical. But I had to face the fact that I am not Superman. I have a lot of weaknesses that I needed to fix up along the way, so I'm not disappointed that I took time to repair them.

Since I've returned, my people tell me that there is something more compassionate in my sermons. I'll often hear, "What you say really touches my heart." My sensitivity is coming back.

—A FOURSQUARE PASTOR

F

Chapter Eleven
Finding Solitude in Sabbaticals

"By the seventh day God completed His work which He had done, and He rested on the seventh day from all His work which He had done. Then God blessed the seventh day and sanctified it."

GENESIS 2:2–3

In our fast-paced, full-scheduled world, taking extended breaks is a luxury afforded only the affluent, old, or sick. It has fallen out of consideration as a vital component to success. But in this chapter, let me persuade you to reconsider the imperative of Sabbath rest. Sabbaths and sabbaticals are biblically designed to increase our fruitfulness and deepen our faith along the way.

The Sabbath is a declaration that God has finished His work of creation. No one needs to add to it, and no one should. God's people were instructed to keep His example by doing nothing to advance their own cause on that day. It was the only aspect

E

of God's creative ability that His creatures could imitate. They could not create, but they could rest. And on the seventh day, God rested.

The Sabbath acknowledges the completed work of God. Violating the Sabbath rest by working is a statement that what we are doing on the Sabbath is as important as what God did at creation. Desisting on the Sabbath simply expresses that our work is insignificant compared to His. Our works—even our ministry activities and other benevolent activities—should always give way to His designs for the day.

We have learned to rest when the work is done. But the fact of the matter is that the work will never be done. There will always be more to do. So the Sabbath rest becomes a command we respond to, not a result of nothing left to do. It is a part of our obedience, not a consequence of our expedience and industriousness.

The work will never be done.

The Jewish people would not only take Sabbaths, but every seventh year they would let the land rest and forgive all debts. They would release any indentured workers and let slaves go free. When Nehemiah returned, he found many of the Israelites violating this once strictly held practice, so he made a new covenant that all the nobles, elders, and people affixed their signatures to. In part, it read:

> When the neighboring peoples bring merchandise or grain to sell on the Sabbath, we will not buy from them on the Sabbath or on any holy day. Every seventh year we will forgo working the land and will cancel all debts. (Nehemiah 10:31 NIV)

SABBATICALS

A sabbatical is like the seventh year. In the Old Testament, it was an extended season to allow the land to regain its potency and allow the soil to restore its nutrients and minerals.

There will likewise be seasons when a sabbatical, or an extended season of rest, becomes crucial to sustaining the shelf life of a minister or Christian leader. It replenishes nutrients to our souls and restores our hunger for life and ministry.

However, a common response to taking a sabbatical is "I just don't have the time." But I'd like you to consider this: "How deep is your hunger and how fruitful is your soul?" These are the critical issues.

PLAYING RIGHT FIELD FOR A SEASON

In October 1993, Michael Jordan bid a tearful good-bye to his Chicago Bulls teammates and set out in a new direction. His team had won three consecutive NBA championships, and "His Airness" had inspired millions of young back-lot basketball hopefuls with his seamless, soaring, Jordan-esque style of play.

The best to ever play the game? Many believed that to be true—and still do.

Just a year earlier, Jordan and his esteemed teammates of the U.S. Dream Team had garnered the gold medal at the Barcelona Olympics. How could there be a greater or more appropriate parting achievement? The Bulls retired number 23 and erected a life-size bronze statue of the famed player outside their United Center.

Sports fans and pundits alike speculated on the reasons for his leaving the game. Perhaps it was the 1993 murder of his father—or maybe the hurtful media spins that he was gambling on NBA games. But two days after his announced retirement, NBA officials closed their probe with a statement that he had committed no wrongdoing.

Jordan, meanwhile, took up the venerated American game of baseball. The six-foot-six point guard signed with the double-A team of the Chicago White Sox early in 1994. But being the hang-time king with the Chicago Bulls was no guarantee that he would become a home-run king with the White Sox.

And he wasn't.

Jordan's batting average was only mediocre, and he spent the majority of his time playing right field—catching fly balls and boosting ticket sales—in Birmingham, Alabama.

Then on March 18, 1995, Jordan returned to the sport he once loved by simply announcing, "I'm back." He donned number 45 and took to the court again. For the next three years he would help the Bulls to gain three more NBA championships, bringing their Jordan-era total to an amazing six. His teammates jokingly said that he still had four more fingers for rings, but on January 13, 1999, Michael Jordan retired (again).

GET YOUR HUNGER BACK

The lesson? The superstar hadn't lost his skills in 1993. He had lost his *hunger*. He knew that if he were going to play basketball, he could only do so with a voracious hunger for the sport. That's what made him excel. That's what would get him up in the mornings. That's what would overcome the obstacles and struggles.

Hunger.

Hunger is renewable.

That's why it may make sense at some point in our lives to play right field for the Birmingham Barons—even if everyone else thinks it's the nuttiest idea in the world.

Sometimes, we may need to get our hunger back.

Hunger is renewable. It may require that you disconnect for a while, do something a little bit different from what you've been used to, but that's okay. It's better than playing the game after the hunger and the desire have faded—just because everyone expects you to.

For Jordan, it was minor-league baseball for two years. For me, it's spending time on a farm in the Northwest. For my friend at the airport, it would be another ministry with new surroundings and new challenges. But whatever it takes, you need to find it. Notice that the former Bulls champion didn't unhook completely from the apparatus of sports. He kept in shape. He practiced. He continued to develop his skills, albeit in a totally different arena.

He didn't need the money or the fame. He needed his hunger back.

My goal was to restore my hunger and passion for what God had called me to do.

Over the years of ministry, I have found that even good ideas get tired. So do good men and women, and when that happens, the endeavor that you are leading is affected. The growth areas are left unattended, the vision flattens, and a leader slowly morphs into a manager. When that happens, you need a break—a break that has one purpose alone: to restore your hunger.

The morph is imperceptible. You won't even recognize the slide, because with energy and passion, you will do far more than you were able, or expected, to do. But when you get tired, you've crossed the Rubicon.

Two weeks before I was to return from my summer break, my wife asked me if I was missing home. Of course I was, but I said, "I'm not quite ready to return yet. My hunger is not back." Within the next two weeks, however, my hunger did return, and I came home ready to go with a vengeance! I had reached my goal of restoring my hunger and passion for what God had called me to do.

LEADERSHIP ENERGY

Think about it: A leader's role is not to maintain. It is to gain altitude! That requires something I call *leadership energy*. Of course, we will always require good managers to keep the gears turning and bearings greased, but only leaders can advance the ministry and give it the significant lift it needs for the future. Leaders need to recognize the growth areas of the ministry and give upward mobility in those areas. Good, dependable managers are worth their weight in gold, but they function optimally only in tandem with leaders, because upward lift and vertical trajectory requires leadership energy.

Approximately one-third of a commercial jet's energy is expended in take-off and gaining altitude. Once they reach 32,000 feet, they maintain altitude, and that requires less energy.

> **A leader needs to give the ministry or company the vertical lift it requires to improve and advance.**

A leader needs to give the ministry or company the vertical lift it requires to improve and advance. Otherwise, over the years, it tends toward entropy. Yesterday's great ideas get tired today, and churches, even great ones, can get tired. Without wise and hungry leaders, a church's endeavors will flatline. Then they end up with lots of programs that do nothing but suck the life out of a ministry.

When a leader returns from a break without getting the hunger back, he or she simply returns to the same-old, same-old. You cannot come back as a manager. You must return a hungry leader. Why? Because the ministry needs a vertical lift and it takes energy and passion for that to happen.

WHY PASTORS NEED SABBATICALS

For many years I would take only Mondays off. However, since I taught a Bible college class on Tuesday mornings, Mondays were dedicated to preparing for the class. And since we have five services on the weekends, Saturdays were given to getting last-minute things ready, and then sound checks had me out of the house by three in the afternoon. So for many years I never had a true Sabbath, because it would always be filled with urgent ministry tasks, which were time-stamped and couldn't be postponed.

When you think about it, in order to enjoy a true Sabbath, you almost need a day to prepare for it! Our Jewish friends taught us that. By Friday night at sundown, Jewish people have all their work done. The house is spotless, the food prepared, the car is washed, and the lawn mowed. Nothing is left undone. Then they enjoy a true Sabbath during the following twenty-four-hour period. Clergy actually could use a two-day Sabbath so the first day could be spent in maintaining their personal lives, and the second could be a true Sabbath rest. However, this seldom happens, and pastors falter in the end.

Not long ago an intern came to serve with us on staff at New Hope for more than a year. At this writing, he has just left to return to his home country in the United Kingdom. Before coming to us, he had sold a business and with his profits moved to Hawaii. Living off his savings, he and his family interned with us, and he took the time and money to renew his hunger. He is now returning to plant a new ministry in his home country.

Another pastor came from Canada on a sabbatical. He and his wife joined us for three months, and while here, he took time to read, rest, spend time with his spouse, and renew his hunger.

He has since returned to Victoria, British Columbia, as a director in his denomination.

A good sabbatical plan includes opportunities for learning. The congregation and board should understand that you learn from other churches as well as from other educational opportunities. The concept of allowing you to visit other churches and attend seminars, conferences, or a seminary class often escapes church boards and the laity in general. Congregational life, technology, and societal norms change rapidly, and the educational opportunities a sabbatical provides ensure that the leadership and the congregation do not end up in a slow, downward spiral to obsolescence.

The educational component, however, should only comprise one-third of the sabbatical. Two-thirds of the time should be cordoned off for a true sabbatical rest—where your vitality is restored with plenty of R&R as well as doing the things that fill your tank.

Some argue that a sabbatical should only begin after seven years. I would concur with that, because it takes that long to get the plane to cruising altitude. But if there are not built-in times to refresh up to that point, the pastor will be the loser in the end. I also believe that long-term pastors should take a three- to four-month break every seven years thereafter.

Some naysayers might react with: "I do not understand why pastors need a sabbatical. I don't get one."

As I said earlier, pastors rarely get a Sabbath day off. Unless they have a large church with multiple pastors on staff, most will put in an eight- to ten-hour day on Sundays. In the marketplace, most workers get at least a two-day weekend. Added to that, most employees in the secular world get about six long weekends a year due to national and state holidays. This means they are off work from late Friday afternoon until Tuesday morning—six times a year.

Now let's apply some basic math. If you multiply these three days off times six weekends, then multiply that number by seven years; it equals 126 days or the equivalent of a three- to four-month sabbatical. In this sense, pastors really don't get any more time off than the average person when they take a sabbatical every seven years.

KEEP HYDRATED

The ideal scenario?

Take drinks "every fifteen minutes" *before* you get thirsty. You will have to fight guilt, and you'll have to overcome the tendency to keep going because you still have the energy. You won't *feel* like you need a drink, but take one anyway.

I have to schedule my breaks at regular intervals whether or not I think I need them. But it keeps my soul hydrated and my heart impassioned. And I still take a break each summer. That's why I prize the great people who faithfully manage the ministry in my absence. They are the ones who keep the gears turning and the bearings greased.

> "Kites rise highest against the wind—not with it."
>
> **WINSTON CHURCHILL**

During the course of my post-burnout life transition, I had to monitor my hunger level. And even now I must keep a close eye on it. My fuel gauge used to remain stuck on **Full**, but no longer. It seems the longer you are in ministry, the "fueling" becomes increasingly more expensive. And one of those investments may require you to break loose for a time.

"But, Wayne," you protest, "how could I even consider such a thing?"

I know. The roadblocks seem pretty intimidating sometimes. Here are a few that come up most often.

Roadblock #1—The Expectations of Others

People's expectations can be merciless.

Recently I traveled for two weeks with a pastor friend of mine, Bill Hybels from Willow Creek Community Church. We team up each year to do leadership forums and training. It's always a rewarding time, and I receive much more than I give out. Bill has been a friend and partner to me for many years.

In the process of our teaching and counseling, we were able to impart training, experiences, and help to over two thousand pastors. Upon my return, I received a letter from a congregant:

> *Dear Wayne:*
>
> *We hear you will be gone again this summer. I am your age also, and I get burned out. I am sure many people do, but we can't just take off. We have to stay and overcome. The best thing you can do is to be here every weekend. We are sure you are paid well by the church to preach full time.*
>
> *I am sure you can come up with tons of reasons why it is important for you to travel, but so could anyone else. You have said your responsibility is to pastor New Hope and spend time with your family. But it seems you are always leaving both. It might just be a distraction that the enemy is using to destroy our church.*

As I have said before, critics are like the poor that Jesus mentions in the Bible: You will always have them with you. But they are the way they are not because they are selfish or evil. It is because they are needy and often immature (which one of us isn't?). However, the agenda shouldn't be driven by the easily offended, so it is our responsibility to say when enough is enough.

Only I can give myself permission to rest or to overachieve, to pace myself or to run at the pace others expect of me.

> "To be right with God has often meant to be in trouble with men."
>
> A. W. TOZER

Imagine a sleepy man entering a small diner in the early morning hours. Still trying to wake up, he orders some strong black coffee. The waitress brings him a cup and saucer, plunks it down in front of him, and begins to pour.

"Just say 'when,'" she says. The man hears her, but his early morning mind isn't fully functioning yet. The server keeps pouring the coffee until it overflows the cup and begins to fill the saucer beneath—and then runs over the top of the saucer across the green Formica table.

Finally, when the steaming liquid spills onto the man's lap, he is jolted to his senses. "Ouch! That's hot! What are you doing?" Like a spooked horse bolting backward, his startled words make the waitress jump.

People's needs are great, and their expectations are endless. You cannot base your life and ministry on the expectations of others.

"I'm so sorry," she says. "But I did tell you to say 'when'. . . ."

The moral to my little parable is simply this: People's needs are great, and their expectations are endless. If you don't say "when," they will drain you. You have to be the one to say, "Whoa! Hold it!" Because if you don't, they certainly won't. It isn't because people are greedy; it is because they are needy. And as much as they love you, no one will monitor your energy level or your personal and emotional health. You will continue to lead on empty, and one day when you lie in the hospital suffering from fatigue and stress, they will say, "Why, he should have taken better care of himself!"

You cannot base your life and ministry on the expectations of others. It will drain you faster than water through a colander.

Roadblock #2—Finances

Taking the time to renew your hunger may mean a break from your regular income stream. For many people, that prospect is a giant roadblock. It's one thing for a multi-millionaire like Michael Jordan to take a break from basketball to play right field in Alabama, but not everyone can afford to forgo salary to recharge their motor.

This is why the best time to negotiate a sabbatical is before you officially begin your ministry in a new congregation. Establishing the terms in advance will help to avoid begging in the end. Request that the church assist you financially during that time if they are able. If they feel the need to hire extra help or pay honorariums for guests to fill in during that time, they can begin a sabbatical savings that will easily cover those costs. Explain to the board or elders the need to stay spiritually vital. It's best to talk about sabbaticals up front. Clarify the details as much as possible, and emphasize the importance of rest so that you can stay healthy and be enthusiastic about the church.

You can explain it in this way: "I believe that the church will benefit the most if every four years, I can take a three-month sabbatical." If this policy is not negotiated up front, you will probably have to wait until you hit the wall. By then, it might be too late. You have to hydrate your soul much sooner than that.

I have found that many churches and ministries provide free housing for pastors on sabbatical. Bible colleges may open a dorm room for the summer, or Christian camps often make a few rooms available for pastors and church leaders to rest for a season. At the end of this book, there is a listing of various camps, retreat centers, and programs available at little or no charge. One excellent ministry for the wounded and burned-out leader is Smoldering Wick Ministries. Smoldering Wick offers free help, including counseling, articles, educational tapes, friendship, and unconditional love.

There are also generous grants available to finance a pastor's sabbatical. One resource can be found online at *www.louisville -institute.org*, or you can contact the Lily Endowment Sabbatical Grant program at their Web site: *www.lillyendowment.org/ religion_ncr.html.*

Roadblock #3—Who Will Lead While I Am Gone?

I wrestled with the question myself. But then I thought, "I have been teaching leadership classes for years, mentoring scores of emerging leaders about managing and problem solving, and now I need to let them LEAD!"

Take a look around you. There are probably board members who can lead—businessmen and women who are fully capable of overseeing the ministry in your absence. I have built a teaching team of pastoral staff, and three individuals rotate giving sermons. Special guests augment that schedule.

I have also built a summer team of teachers and key leaders who know that they will have a six-week run in the summer to lead. I ask them to prepare a series on increasing our sense of community and to deepen our fellowship. They have all year to think through that six-week series that is geared to increase relationships, teach people how to problem solve, and strengthen unity in the church. They can do small groups on that theme, have picnics, movie nights, or whatever they feel is appropriate.

Directly after the weekend we celebrate Father's Day (which is the third Sunday in June), I leave on my study break. Then the team enjoys six weeks without me breathing over their shoulders, and they can lead to their heart's content! And that gives me six weeks to plan my next year, to spend time with my family, and. . .

Ride my motorcycle.

ASKING THE RIGHT QUESTIONS

I will meditate with my heart, and my spirit ponders. (Psalm 77:6)

When you go on a sabbatical, in order to gain clarity, take with you life questions to ponder before God. Renewing your energy and revitalizing your life will require seasons of self-assessment. No, not *introspection*, but rather times when you ask questions that will guide your future choices. God has designed your mind in such a way that if you feed it the right questions, your imagination will be unlocked and a God-inspired inner mechanism is ignited. This is when creative problem solving begins and your subconscious starts seeking ways to solve dilemmas and rectify imbalances. David reminded me that God would stir my soul and instruct me even while I slept! My inner thought processes are working if I ask the right questions:

I will bless the Lord who has counseled me; indeed, my mind instructs me in the night. (Psalm 16:7)

Prayer is thinking deeply about something in the presence of God.

Let me suggest to you a definition of prayer: *Prayer is thinking deeply about something in the presence of God.* It may include intercession, but it is far more than that. It is in discussing these things with the Holy Spirit that we receive understanding and insight.

The questions you pose to yourself will be absolutely critical. Some questions will come naturally, but others will need to be prepared and intentional. Gordon MacDonald, in his great book *A Resilient Life*, suggests what we will naturally ask as we grow older:[1]

30s

When I reached my 30s, my life questions were about marriage, children, bills, housing, and fulfillment.

- How do I cope with the demands being made on me? (Talk to a young mother about her quiet times and see her laugh at you.)

- Why do I often feel that I cannot please anyone? How far can I go in fulfilling my dreams?

- Where did all my old friends go? (Most of our best friendships happen before we reach 20.)

- Why am I not a better person?

40s

When you are in your 40s, the questions seem to circle around life issues such as:

- Who was I as a child and what influences shaped me?

- Why do some people seem to be doing better than me?

- Why am I so disappointed in others and myself?

- Why are my limitations seemingly outpacing my strengths?

- Am I making a contribution? Am I making a difference?

50s

Things change when you reach 50. Your body doesn't do what it used to. You see younger, more talented people rising everywhere, and you try to hold on to what you have. You tend to be more conservative and you risk less. Questions you grapple with may resemble the following:

- Why is time moving so fast?

- Why don't I have the time to do all the things I want to do?

- Why is my body becoming so unreliable?

- How do I deal with my failures and successes?

- How do my spouse and I adjust to the changes in our marriage?
- Why do young people seem to want to replace me?
- Will I have enough money for retirement?
- What do I do with the fears I have?

60s

In your 60s, the questions turn toward the past and to the future:

- When do I stop doing the things that have defined me?
- How can I slow down my pace without feeling unnecessary anymore?
- Why do I feel ignored by such a large part of the population?
- What is my spiritual legacy?
- What can I yet accomplish?
- What does old age feel like and am I ready for it?

70s and 80+

In this final stage, our thoughts turn toward legacy and eternity:

- Will anyone know who I once was?
- How much of my life can I still control?
- Will I allow others to have that control?
- What can I contribute?
- Is God really there for me?
- Am I ready to face dying?
- When I go, will anyone miss me after a few days?

PREPARING CORRECTLY

Taking a sabbatical is usually because of the need to reassess. It is also often birthed out of pain. So if you do not prepare the right questions to ask, your discouraged mind will ask self-defeating ones. Avoid these at all costs. Some debilitating questions may include:

1. Why did God allow me to go through this?
2. Why didn't He stop me?
3. Do I have enough money to retire *now*?
4. What other jobs can I get?
5. I need a break from my marriage. Does God have someone else for me?

"When one door closes, another opens; but we often look so long and so regretfully upon the closed door that we do not see the one which has opened for us."

ALEXANDER GRAHAM BELL

Questions like these will plague your mind and defeat you. Do not allow yourself questions that only fish for suicidal answers. Here's the danger: The more you think about them, the more plausible they seem. You begin to feel defeated and depressed. Solomon reminds us all to choose the questions we bring up in Ecclesiastes 5:2:

> Do not be hasty in word or impulsive in thought to bring up a matter in the presence of God. For God is in heaven and you are on the earth; therefore let your words be few.

God doesn't discourage questions. He is simply encouraging us not to allow poor questions to taint our perspectives and soil our dispositions before we even come to Him!

QUESTIONS TO ASK IN A SEASON OF SELF-ASSESSMENT:

1. **What was my original calling from God?** Take time to answer this one as fully as you are able. Write down the major components to this calling. How has it changed over the years? Is it still valid? What parts of it might have morphed into something else? Do you need to reinvent yourself in order to return to this assignment?

> When depression hits, look at your divine commission and say, "That is where I need to start again."

2. **What activities that I am involved in do I love the most?** List the things that you love to do. Be very honest here. Don't write things down that you only do because they are expected of you. Write down the things you think and dream about.

3. **What activities and people have been draining my tank?** Identify both the activities *and* the people. If you are a leader of any endeavor, you must think through how to resolve unnecessary drain in order to replenish the energy levels that were there in the beginning.

4. **If I retired today with several million dollars and no debts, what would I do?** This might be reality for some and theoretical for most. In either case, if you were independently wealthy, what would you do with your time that would fully utilize your gifts and make a contribution to mankind in the name of Christ? What would excite you and wake you up each morning? What would that kind of life look like on a daily basis? What would be your ideal lifestyle—not in leisure, but in serving the purposes of God in your

generation? What would make it "Christmas every day" for you? Here are a few cautions:

a. Do not list anything that you couldn't do with all your heart.

b. Do not list anything that you couldn't do deeply and enjoy.

c. Be sure that your list includes your highest-priority relationships in life: your relationship with God, your spouse, your family, your church, and your community.

What can you see yourself doing that would so fill you that you could do it until Jesus returns? Instead of waiting until you retire, begin to set in motion a systematic way to do these things within the next five years by slightly transitioning your life to include those activities and relationships now.

5. **What triggered my depletion?** Write down what you think may have caused your burnout.

6. **What am I doing now that I cannot do anymore?** What activities and tasks are you doing that you must immediately delegate to others? List them and evaluate each one to see which ones must be pruned immediately and which ones must go eventually. Give timelines to each.

7. **What are those things that I enjoy doing but cannot do to the level I am involved now?** John 15:2 says: "Every branch in Me that does not bear fruit, He takes away; and *every branch that bears fruit, He prunes it so that it may bear more fruit*" (emphasis added).

"You are now at a crossroads. This is your opportunity to make the most important decision you will ever make. Forget your past. Who are you now? . . . Who have you decided to become? Make this decision consciously. Make it carefully. Make it powerfully."

ANTHONY ROBBINS

In order to gain a more fruitful future, there may be some things you enjoy that are not necessarily a part of your assignment. These need to be pruned back.

8. **Who do I need to share these findings with so that the rebuilding can begin?**

These simple questions will begin your journey to health and a new beginning. You have suffered much and you have learned much. In due time God will use you in mighty ways to help others navigate the same waters. You have a wealth of wisdom that was deposited to your account at a high price. And now your greatest days lie ahead of you.

> "Many of life's failures are people who did not realize how close they were to success when they gave up."
>
> **THOMAS EDISON**

You are poised to be a mentor, a coach, a more gracious and understanding person. These will be your best years. Walk forward with confidence.

The kingdom of God awaits you.

Afterword

Here, in summary, is probably the most important part of this book.

As I write these final paragraphs, I am recuperating from heart surgery performed last week at Stanford Medical Hospital in Menlo Park, California. Three blocked arteries required me to leave Hawaii for California immediately for a procedure performed by an exemplary surgeon. I am feeling much better today and *resilience* bids me forward.

These lessons learned do not mean I will shrink back. Rather, it means that I will live much more deeply, with far more security. I will laugh more often, think with more insight, and find moments of solitude and Sabbath without guilt.

I have walked through a long season. I have learned many lessons. I have discovered what is most important: how to live intentionally and how to run with hope. I have learned the importance of being utterly committed to the truth and how to be honest about who I am.

I have also learned the importance of coaching more and doing less. Two men impacted my journey:

The first is Bob Buford, who wrote to me after my surgery and reminded me of what Peter Drucker, the great business strategist, once told him:

> This is a season for you to direct and release energy rather than supply it.

The other is Tom Paterson, whom I referred to in chapter 9. He wrote me a note during my search for direction. In it he concluded:

> When a person actually burns out, he goes through a metamorphosis, a change in substance, character, and appearance. He cannot successfully go back to what he was doing. It seems to me that you have experienced actual burnout, and that is why simply taking six weeks off to rehab did not work.
>
> It is time now to invest the rest of your life in what the Lord was preparing you for with the experience you have had. Your new work life should find you doing only those things that you feel very passionate about.

WHAT LIES AHEAD?

I feel like a football player who has been playing hard for many consecutive seasons. And now I must retire from *playing* football, but not necessarily from football itself. I am now open for coaching positions, and my first invitation is to coach the team that I have been playing with for these past twenty-five years. I realize that my greatest discipline will be to overcome the temptation to put on pads again and hit the gridiron.

I have spent many hours deciding what I am passionate about and what I can spend the rest of my days doing. It will be within the inviolable grid of what's most important, and within those guardrails, I now run with hope.

WHAT LIES WITHIN?

Your greatest source of motivation is finding untapped potential yet within you. You see, your future is not what lies ahead of you. It is what lies within you.

Potential is everything you can be but haven't become yet. It is everything you can do but haven't done yet. It's everywhere you can go but haven't gone yet. Potential is the books you can write that you haven't written yet. It is the life you've wanted to live but haven't lived yet. It is like a huge engine—running idle. It is energy still underutilized, power yet unleashed, and strength yet unused.

> ## Potential is everything you can be but haven't become yet.

When your potential is tapped-out in the place you have been, it may require another location to uncork potential that lies latent within. Other times, it may require a new vision or a renewed cause that you've lost sight of. But whatever the direction may be, find that new potential!

Potential always lies ahead of you, not behind you. It is found in what can still be done, not in what you have already done.

I noticed that about Paul the apostle. Although older and in prison, facing the possibility of death, he garners a renewed energy to continue with vitality and buoyancy. Where does he garner this energy?

Philippians 3:12 gives it away: "I press on so that I may lay hold of that for which also I was laid hold of by Christ Jesus."

Your past may be filled with trophies or checkered with failure, but in either case, evaluate what you can yet improve on and what you can still accomplish. Imagine what would excite you and awaken you each morning. What cadence and what pace will help you attain and *maintain* joy?

When you begin to dream in that way, you will find a brand-new hope. And when you discover that, write it down and follow it. Find your potential. It will be there, within the wrappings of your passion and packaged within holy parameters.

Through the vale of burnout, find out who you are. Surrender. Because when you do, your best days will await your arrival.

Notes

Foreword

1. Adapted and used with permission from Bob Buford, *Beyond Halftime* (Grand Rapids, MI: Zondervan, 2009).

Chapter 2

1. H.B. London Jr. and Neil B. Wiseman, *Pastors at Greater Risk* (Ventura, CA: Regal Books, 2003), 20, 86, 118, 148, 172, 264.

Chapter 3

1. "Why Am I So Depressed?" Brenda Poinsett, *Discipleship Journal*, Issue #121, January/February 2001, NavPress.

2. Mother Teresa and Rev. Brian Kolodiejchuk, *Mother Teresa: Come Be My Light* (New York: Doubleday, 2007).

3. Gilbert Thomas, *William Cowper and the Eighteenth Century* (London: Ivor Nicholson and Watson Ltd., 1935), 131–32.

4. Retrieved from *www.stempublishing.com/hymns/biographies/cowper.html*.

5. *The Minister's Fainting Fits*, Charles Spurgeon, Lecture XL, retrieved from *www.the-highway.com/articleSept99.html*.

6. Dr. Darrel W. Amundsen, "The Anguish and Agonies of Charles Haddon Spurgeon," *Christian History*, Issue #29, 1991.

7. Ibid.

8. Ibid.

9. *The Writings of Abraham Lincoln, Volume 1*, Abraham Lincoln research site, *http://www.att.net/~rjnorton/Lincoln84.html*

Chapter 8

1. Taken from Christine and Tom Sine, *Living on Purpose: Finding God's Best for Your Life* (Grand Rapids, MI: Baker Books, 2002), 17.

Chapter 11

1. Adapted from Gordon MacDonald, *A Resilient Life* (Nashville, TN: Thomas Nelson, Inc., 2004), 53–58.

Appendix

RETREAT CENTERS AND COUNSELORS

Many of these retreat centers are free. You pay your travel expenses. These are committed people who love pastors and leaders, and they understand burnout and depression. Often denominational facilities are available, and during the summer months many Bible colleges will make their dormitories available for the asking.

The following is for informational purposes only. I don't necessarily have enough personal experience to endorse them all.

1. *www.smolderingwickministries.org*; OK, $150 a day
2. *www.pastorsretreatnetwork.org*; WI, TX, OH; Free to qualifying pastors
3. *www.coronadocottage.org*; San Diego, CA; Partial scholarships available
4. *www.retreatsonline.com/guide/christian.htm*; U.S., Canada, UK, Europe
5. *http://pastorforlife.org/pastor-retreat-centers/*; WI, CA, FL, CO, GA, TX, TN, Canada

6. *www.nazarenepastor.org/cms/Default.aspx?tabid=120*; Multiple centers listed by Free/Inexpensive; U.S., Canada, Mexico, Germany, Africa

7. *http://ccpastors.org/retreats.html*; TN, WA, IL, OR, WI, MI

8. *www.osb.org/retreats/*; U.S., Canada, UK, France, Italy

9. *www.dayspringretreat.org*; MD; $45 overnight

10. *www.sbcamping.org*; Multiple U.S. centers listed by regions

11. *www.Lakedon.org*; Kansas City

12. *http://ag.org/top/ministers/Development/retreats.pdf*; Multiple U.S. centers listed by states

13. *www.dmoz.org/Society/Religion_and_Spirituality/Christianity/Camps_and_Retreats/*; Multiple camps listed by Denomination/Non-denominations; Retreat centers

14. *www.sonscape.com*; CO, GA; Sliding fee scale and scholarships

15. *www.findthedivine.com/*; Over 1,700 retreat centers

16. *www.parsonage.org/events/PSR.cfm*; Focus on the Family, The Parsonage

SOME BOOKS TO CHECK FOR FURTHER OPTIONS:

1. *Going on Retreat: A Beginner's Guide to the Christian Retreat Experience,* Margaret Silf, September 2002

2. *A Place for God—A Guide to Spiritual Retreats and Retreat Centers,* Timothy Jones, 2000

3. *Handbook for Great Camps and Retreats,* Chap Clark, May 2004

4. *U.S. and Worldwide Guide to Retreat Center Guest Houses,* John Jensen, June 1997 (Out of print, limited supply)

5. *Catholic America: Self-Renewal Centers and Retreats,* Patricia Christian-Meyer, January 1993 (Out of print, limited supply)

6. *Traveler's Guide to Healing Centers and Retreats in North America,* Martine Rudee, April 1989 (Out of print, limited supply)

COUNSELORS:

1. International Association of Christian Counseling Professionals: *www.iaccp.net/*

2. Focus on the Family—U.S. counseling referral database for varying specialties; Counseling Dept.; Canadian Affiliate Office: *http://family.custhelp.com/cgi-bin/family.cfg/php/enduser/std_adp.php?p_faqid=13&p_created*

3. American Association of Christian Counselors Referral Network: *www.aacc.net/*

4. National Christian Counselors Association: *www.ncca.org/*

5. Mentoring for Pastors' Wives: *http://biblecounselor.com/pastorswives.html*

6. Link Care Center for Pastoral Restoration Services: *www.linkcare.org/lc_services_pastoral.php*

7. 711 Christian Directory: *http://search.711.net/Church_-_Pastoral_Resources/Counseling/*

8. Minirth Meier New Life Clinic—The Day Spring Center: *www.minirth-meier-newlife.com/*

9. Samaritan Counseling Services, Ann Arbor, MI: *www.samaritan.cc/*

10. Cleanwaters Counseling Ministries for Pastors: *www.cleanwaterscounseling.com/CounselingforPastorsMinistersandtheirfamilies.dsp*

Books for the Journey

Ruth Barton, *Invitation to Solitude and Silence* (Downer's Grove, IL: InterVarsity Press, 2004).

Henry Cloud and John Townsend, *Boundaries* (Grand Rapids, MI: Zondervan, 1992).

Verdell Davis, *Let Me Grieve, But Not Forever* (Nashville: Thomas Nelson, 1994).

James Dobson, *When God Doesn't Make Sense* (Carol Stream, IL: Tyndale House, 1994).

Emerson Eggerichs, *Love and Respect* (Brentwood, TN: Integrity, 2004).

John Eldredge, *Waking the Dead* (Nashville, TN: Thomas Nelson, 2003).

Richard J. Foster, *Freedom of Simplicity* (New York: HarperCollins, 1981).

Richard J. Foster and James Bryan Smith, editors, *Devotional Classics* (San Francisco: HarperSanFrancisco, 1993).

Ken Gire, *Intimate Moments With the Savior* (Grand Rapids, MI: Zondervan, 1989).

Ken Gire, *The Reflective Life* (Colorado Springs: Cook Communications, 1998).

Archibald D. Hart, *The Hidden Link Between Adrenaline and Stress* (Nashville, TN: Thomas Nelson, 1995).

Archibald D. Hart, *Unmasking Male Depression* (Nashville: Thomas Nelson, 2001).

Archibald D. Hart, *A Woman's Guide to Overcoming Depression* (Grand Rapids, MI: Baker Publishing Group, 2007); previously published as *Unveiling Depression in Women* (Grand Rapids, MI: Baker Publishing Group, 2002).

Jack Hayford, *Pastors of Promise* (Ventura, CA: Gospel Light, 1998).

Robert Hemfelt, Frank Minirth, and Paul Meier, *Love Is a Choice* (Nashville: Thomas Nelson, 1989).

Anne Jackson, *Mad Church Disease* (Grand Rapids, MI: Zondervan, 2009).

Gordon MacDonald, *A Resilient Life: You Can Move Ahead No Matter What* (Nashville: Thomas Nelson, 2006).

Brennan Manning, *Abba's Child* (Colorado Springs: NavPress, 1994).

Brennan Manning, *A Glimpse of Jesus* (New York: HarperCollins, 2003).

Henri Nouwen, *Heart Speaks to Heart* (Notre Dame, IN: Ave Maria Press, 1989).

John Ortberg, *God Is Closer Than You Think* (Grand Rapids, MI: Zondervan, 2005).

John Ortberg, *The Life You've Always Wanted* (Grand Rapids, MI: Zondervan, 1997).

Tom Paterson, *Living the Life You Were Meant to Live* (Nashville: Thomas Nelson, 1998).

Eugene Peterson, *Working the Angles* (Grand Rapids, MI: Eerdmans, 1987).

Naomi Quenk, *In the Grip* (Oxford, England: Oxford Psychologists Press, 1996).

Robert Quinn, *Deep Change* (San Francisco: Wiley, 1996).

Peter Scazzero, *The Emotionally Healthy Church* (Grand Rapids, MI: Zondervan, 2003).

Margaret Silf, *Going on Retreat: A Beginner's Guide to the Christian Retreat Experience* (Chicago: Loyola Press, 2002).

Douglas Weiss, *Intimacy* (Lake Mary, FL: Siloam Press, 2003).

Dallas Willard, *Hearing God* (Downer's Grove, IL: InterVarsity Press, 1999).

Philip Yancey, *Disappointment With God* (Grand Rapids, MI: Zondervan, 1988).

Philip Yancey, *Where Is God When It Hurts?* (Grand Rapids, MI: Zondervan, 1990).

About the Author

WAYNE CORDEIRO is founder and senior pastor of New Hope Christian Fellowship in Honolulu, Hawaii, one of the nation's fastest growing churches. Wayne is an author, songwriter, and highly sought-after conference speaker around the world. His books include *The Divine Mentor, Doing Church as a Team,* and *Attitudes That Attract Success.* He is a church planter at heart and has helped to plant over 100 churches in the Pacific Rim. Wayne and his wife, Anna, have three children and live in Honolulu.

Capture God's promises
as well as the counsel of
divine mentors as you
meet with them in your
daily devotions.

The "Life Calendar" is
designed to prompt you
to obedience in the area of
prayer, relationships and life
essentials. This tool will help you
become all you were meant to be!

290 Sand Island Access Road
Honolulu, HI 96819
808-842-4242

Contact us at
info@lifejournal.cc
with any questions.

For a FREE CATALOG or for
more information, check out
www.lifejournal.cc

MORE OF THE BEST
FROM WAYNE CORDEIRO

The Divine Mentor
Growing Your Faith as You
Sit at the Feet of your Savior

Doing Church As A Team
The Miracle of Teamwork and
How It Transforms Churches

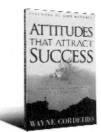

Attitudes That Attract Success
You're Only One Attitude Away
from a GREAT Life!

Culture Shift
Transforming Your Church
from the Inside Out

The Dream Releasers
How to Help Others Realize Their
Dreams While Achieving Your Own

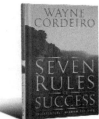

The Seven Rules of Success
Indispensible Wisdom for Life

Pick up a copy at your favorite Christian Bookstore, today!	Contact us at **info@lifejournal.cc** with any questions.	For a FREE CATALOG or for more information, check out **www.lifejournal.cc**

More From Wayne Cordeiro

Revive Your Quiet Time
Discover how to enjoy a dynamic, vital, and intimate relationship with God as you learn to hear Him speak daily through the Bible. With this excellent guide to daily quiet times, you'll embark on an adventure that will introduce you to His handpicked mentors—biblical men and women—who may save your health, your marriage, your ministry, and your future.

The Divine Mentor by Wayne Cordeiro

"Wayne Cordeiro's message and ministry are a gift to the kingdom of God. I'm confident his book will be an encouragement to all who read it."

—Max Lucado, bestselling author

"When it comes to diving into the Book and letting God talk to me through its message, no one has mentored me more than Wayne Cordeiro."

—Bill Hybels, Senior Pastor, Willow Creek Community Church